The Great Chocolate Book

The Great Chocolate Book

Marvellous chocolate recipes from the finest restaurants in Great Britain and Ireland

Absolute Press

Published by Absolute Press (publishers)
14 Widcombe Crescent, Widcombe Hill, Bath, Avon.
Tel: (0225) 316013

First published November 1986
Reprinted November 1988

© Absolute Press

Editor **Paula Borton**

Illustrations **Joe Mallia**

Cover printed by
Stopside Ltd, Windsor Bridge Road, Bath.

Phototypeset by
Sulis Typesetting, 2 Gay Street, Bath.

Printed by
WBC Print, Barton Manor, St. Philips, Bristol.

Bound by WBC Bookbinders, Maesteg.

Contents

Introduction

In the early part of the sixteenth century, when Cortez returned from Mexico laden with the fruits of the cacao plant, he could have little realised the effect that his discovery from the new world would have upon the old. Over the next two hundred and fifty years the chocolate drink became a fashionable and essential part of first Spanish, then Italian and French and finally English social life. The pioneering developments of people such as Joseph Fry and Rudolph Lindt meant that during the nineteenth century eating chocolate was produced, and with it one of the most profitable industries in the world. Its appearance caused an immediate sensation and the first chocoholics became addicted. The publication of The Great Chocolate Book is a testimony to the fact that chocolate has lost nothing of its appeal and indeed continues to beguile and seduce innocent victims.

The recipes in The Great Chocolate Book are the aristocrats of chocolate cuisine. Wonderful recipes from the great restaurant kitchens of Great Britain and Ireland. Not for the faint-hearted or the novice, these are recipes to satisfy even the most hardened of chocoholics.

Types of chocolate

Plain & bitter chocolate

Both plain and bitter chocolate are excellent for cooking
and have a strong and intense flavour.

Milk chocolate

The cocoa content of milk chocolate is less than plain
chocolate and thus has a less intense flavour and will result
in less rich dishes.

White chocolate

Not in fact a chocolate at all, being made from milk, sugar
and cocoa butter and containing no chocolate liquor.

Chocolate Couverture

A chocolate much used by professional chefs who favour it
for its excellent cooking and spreading qualities. Hard to
obtain but well worth acquiring should you discover a
source of supply.

Savoury

Suprème de Pigeonneau au chocolat Amer et sa cuisse en Ronselle

French Partridge, Horton
Chef/proprietor David Partridge

Serves 1

1 pigeon
1 oz. (25g.) minced pork
1 oz. (25g.) onion, finely
  chopped
1 fl. oz. (25ml.) cream
puff pastry
bitter chocolate
salt and pepper

Carefully remove the pigeon breasts.

Use the carcass to make a good flavoured stock.

Remove the carcass and pick off leg meat and shred finely. Continue reducing the stock and de-grease.

Fry the pork in a frying pan. Add the onion, seasoning and a pinch of mixed herbs. When the onion is soft, add the prepared leg meat and allow to cool.

Roll out a circle of pastry and half fill with the mixture. Seal the edges and glaze with beaten egg. Bake at 400F/200C/Gas 6 for approximately 15 minutes.

Fry the seasoned breasts both sides – they should be pink.

De-glaze the pan with the reduced stock and cream. Finish the sauce by adding a square of bitter chocolate and whisking in. Serve the pigeons accompanied by the pastry turnover and the sauce.

Grilled Breast of Duck with Chocolate Sauce and Parsnip and Watercress Purée

Morels, Haslemere
Chef/proprietor J. Morel

Serves 2

1 large duck
1 onion, chopped
2 carrots, chopped
½ cup sherry vinegar
bouquet garni
1 pint (570ml.) veal stock
½ pint (275ml.) water
1 oz. (25g.) bitter chocolate

For the purée:

7 oz. (200g.) parsnip, cooked till
  soft
bunch watercress, blanched
salt and pepper

Remove the legs from the duck and set aside for use in another dish. Roast the breasts on the carcass for 5 minutes until the fat starts to run out. Cool and take the breast meat off the carcass – try to keep the breasts in one piece.

Make a stock by chopping up the bones and roasting till brown in the oven. Place in a pot, add the chopped vegetables and bouquet garni – be sure to sweat the vegetables in a little oil or butter before adding to the pot. Pour in the sherry vinegar and deglaze. Add the veal stock and water and cook for 40–60 minutes. Strain and reduce by half. Take off the heat and stir in the chocolate. Put this sauce to one side.

Grill the partly cooked breasts lightly, carve into slices and pour the sauce around. Arrange the purée on the plate to best effect.

Bécasse Rôtie au Vinaigre de Framboise et Chocolat

Restaurant Bosquet, Kenilworth
Chef/proprietor Bernard Lignier

1 woodcock per person
2 shallots
1½ oz. (40g.) back fat
1 piece toast per bird
1 tablespoon brandy
2 oz. (50g.) butter
1½ oz. (40g.) foie gras or
  chicken liver

For the sauce:

1 sherry glass raspberry
  vinegar
1 sherry glass port
2 sherry glasses of demi-glace
½ oz. (15g.) bitter chocolate
1 oz. (25g.) butter

Cover the woodcock with a thin layer of back fat, pinch the legs together with the beak, season and cook in a hot oven for 5 minutes. Discard the back fat, remove the guts and reserve them (discarding the gizzard) and return the bird to the oven for a further 5 minutes. It should be pink inside.

Make the rotie by liquidising the guts with the butter, shallots, brandy, salt and pepper and foie gras or chicken liver. When smooth, place on a slice of bread, toasted on both sides, and grill slowly.

Make the sauce by boning the bird and placing the breasts and legs on the toasted rotie with the head of the bird split in two. Place the left over bones in the roasting dish, deglaze with the raspberry vinegar, port and demi-glace. Stir in the chocolate and bring to the boil and reduce by half. Pass through a fine sieve and add the butter.

Royal Recipe for Hare

Michael's, Bristol
Chef/proprietor Michael McGowan

1 hare
butter to cook

For the marinade:

½ pint (275ml.) white wine
2 carrots, chopped
2 onions, chopped
1 head celery, chopped
1 clove garlic, chopped
bay leaf
3 cloves, bunch parsley, fresh
   thyme

For the sauce:

1 oz. (25g.) caster sugar
1 tablespoon wine vinegar
2 oz. (50g.) pine nuts
1 oz. (25g.) currants
2 oz. (50g.) bitter chocolate,
   grated

Joint the hare. Place the pieces in the marinade and leave for 12 hours, turning occasionally.

Take the hare out of the marinade and dry the pieces with kitchen paper. Put the marinade into another saucepan and place over a heat. Heat the butter in a large saucepan and fry the meat until lightly browned. Add the hot marinade to the meat and cover. Simmer, or cook in the oven, for about 1 hour or until the hare is cooked.

Make the sauce, by caramelising the sugar with a teaspoon of water in a small pan. Add the wine vinegar and leave to cool. When the hare is done, strain off the liquid and keep the meat warm. Add half of the juices to the sugar/vinegar with the nuts and the chocolate. Bring the sauce to the boil, stirring all the while. Carve the meat onto a large platter and pour over the sauce. Garnish with something green and serve with plain boiled rice, potatoes or pasta.

Le Filet de Lièvre au Vinaigre de Framboises et au Chocolat Amer

La Tante Claire, London
Chef/proprietor Pierre Koffman

4 fillets hare
1 teaspoon chopped shallot
18 fl. oz. (½ litre) red wine
5 fl. oz. (150ml.) veal stock
1 fl. oz. (25ml.) raspberry
  vinegar
2 cubes bitter chocolate
salt and pepper

Season the fillets and cook in a frying pan, keeping them pink in the middle. Remove to a plate and allow to rest.

In the same pan, having thrown away the fat, sweat the shallots. Deglaze with the vinegar and let it reduce completely. Add the wine and let it reduce to ⅓ of its original quantity. Add the stock and the chocolate. When the chocolate has melted add a little nut of butter to thicken the sauce.

Slice the fillets of hare and arrange on a serving plate in the shape of a fan. Pour the sauce on top.

Hot

Rich Chocolate Sauce

Thornbury Castle, Thornbury
Chef Colin Hingston

3½ oz. (100g.) dark chocolate
1¼ oz. (30g.) unsalted butter
5 tablespoons water
2 tablespoons rum, brandy or
  Grand Marnier

This excellent all-purpose rich chocolate sauce can be served either hot or cold and can be adapted by replacing the water with cream for a different texture.

To make the chocolate sauce, simply heat all the ingredients together in a bain-marie until a smooth sauce forms.

Hot Chocolate Soufflé

Thornbury Castle, Thornbury
Chef Colin Hingston

Serves 8

juice 1 orange and finely grated
    zest
12 oz. (350g.) good dark
    chocolate
6 oz. (175g.) unsalted butter
6 egg yolks
2½ fl. oz. (65ml.) dark rum
2½ fl. oz. (65ml.) strong coffee
6 egg whites
2 oz. (50g.) caster sugar

Place the first six ingredients into a double saucepan and gently heat over water until the yolks are cooked. Remove from the heat and leave to cool.

When almost cold, whisk the egg whites and sugar to a meringue and fold into the chocolate. Pour into greased soufflé dishes and bake in a low oven until risen – about 20 minutes.

Hot Chocolate Soufflé

Corse Lawn House, Corse Lawn
Chef/proprietor Baba Hine

6 eggs separated
1 pint (570ml.) milk
3 oz. (75g.) sugar
3 oz. (75g.) chocolate powder

Cream together the egg yolks, sugar and chocolate powder.

Bring the milk to the boil, add slowly to the mixture and cook gently over a low heat until the mixture coats the back of a spoon. Allow to cool.

Whip the egg whites until stiff and fold in the chocolate custard mixture. Pour into individual ramekin dishes and cook in a fairly hot oven 400F/200C/Gas 6 for about 8 minutes. Serve immediately.

Chocolate and Almond Soufflé

Gidleigh Park, Chagford
Chef Shaun Hill

Serves 4

4 oz. (125g.) plain chocolate
2 tablespoons milk
3½ oz. (100g.) caster sugar
2 oz. (50g.) ground almonds
1 tablespoon flour
5 fl. oz. (150ml.) double cream
4 eggs, separated

Butter a 1 pint (570ml.) soufflé dish.

Gently melt the chocolate with the milk.

Whisk the 4 egg yolks and sugar till creamy white.

Sift the ground almonds and flour. Whisk into the egg yolk mixture and then add the chocolate and cream.

Whisk the egg whites until stiff and then fold into the mixture. Pour into soufflé dish and bake at 400F/200C/Gas 6 for 30 minutes.

Chocolate Soufflé Pudding

Cannons, Bath
Chef Raymond Duthie

Serves 6

2¼ oz. (55g.) sugar
3 oz. (75g.) sifted flour
3 oz. (75g.) unsalted butter
8 fl. oz. (225ml.) milk
4 eggs
4½ oz. (135g.) bitter chocolate
½ vanilla pod
pinch salt
white chocolate sauce

Place the milk over a medium heat and bring to the boil with the vanilla pod. Remove from the heat and add the chocolate stirring continuously until dissolved.

Cream the butter and blend in the flour. Pour the hot milk over the butter and flour and mix till smooth. Dry out over the heat till the mixture leaves the sides of the pan. Remove from the heat and add the sugar, a pinch of salt and the egg yolks. When the consistency of a thick custard is reached, work in ⅓ of the stiffly whipped egg whites till completely absorbed. Gently fold in the other ⅔. Divide the mixture between 6 individual soufflé dishes (which have been well greased and lined with sugar) filling them ¾ full.

Bake in a bath of hot water in a fairly hot oven without allowing the water to boil, for approximately 20–25 minutes. Cover the top of the puddings with oiled greaseproof paper when the top has become sufficiently coloured. Remove from the oven and allow to stand for a few minutes. Turn out onto a pool of hot white chocolate sauce.

Steamed Chocolate Pudding

Flowers, Bath
Chef/proprietor Teresa Lipin

Serves 6

5 oz. (150g.) bitter chocolate
7½ oz. (215g.) fresh white
    breadcrumbs
3 oz. (75g.) butter
3 oz. (75g.) caster sugar
7 fl. oz. (200ml.) milk
3 eggs
few drops vanilla essence
pinch cinnamon

Cut the chocolate into small pieces and dissolve slowly in the milk.

Cream the butter in a basin and sieve the sugar on top. Add the yolks and a few of the breadcrumbs and mix well. Then add the chocolate, vanilla essence, cinnamon and the rest of the crumbs. Mix again.

Whip the egg whites to a stiff froth and fold lightly into the rest of the mixture. Pour the mixture into a well greased mould and cover with greased paper. Place the mould in a large saucepan with about 1″ (2.5cm.) of water in it and steam the pudding, semi-covered, gently for about 1 hour or until it has risen and feels firm to the touch. Serve with thick cream.

Steamed White Chocolate Pudding with Dark Chocolate and Rum Sauce

Homewood Park, Hinton Charterhouse
Chef/proprietor Stephen Ross

4 oz. (125g.) sugar
4 oz. (125g.) butter
2 beaten eggs
4 oz. (125g.) plain flour
pinch of salt
3 oz. (75g.) white chocolate
2 tablespoons milk
teaspoon of vanilla

For the sauce:

8 oz. (225g.) plain chocolate
8 oz. (225g.) caster sugar
½ pint (275ml.) water
2 tablespoons rum

Melt the white chocolate in a double boiler or in a pan over simmering water.

Cream the butter and sugar until fluffy, add the beaten eggs, flour and salt, and beat thoroughly. Fold in the melted white chocolate and add enough milk to give a dropping consistency. Pour into a 2 pint (1.1 litre) greased pudding basin and cover with grease-proof paper. Steam for 1½–2 hours.

To make the sauce, grate the chocolate very finely. Boil the sugar in the water until dissolved and syrupy. Stir in the grated chocolate and cook, preferably in a double saucepan over a very low heat till the chocolate has melted. Stir in the rum.

Chocolate Pudding with Blood Orange Sauce

Fischer's, Bakewell
Chef/proprietor Max Fischer

Serves 10

For the pudding:

3½ oz. (100g.) dark chocolate
   couverture
6 egg yolks
3½ oz. (100g.) sugar
vanilla from one pod
3½ oz. (100g.) ground almonds
2 oz. (50g.) fine breadcrumbs
6 egg whites

For the orange sauce:

8 blood oranges, 5 segmented,
   3 for juice only
1 tablespoon cornflour

Use either 10 individual moulds or 1 large cake mould. Brush out with melted butter and dust with icing sugar.

Melt the chocolate in a bain-marie. Add the egg yolk, vanilla and half the sugar and whisk. Whisk the egg whites separately with the remaining sugar until stiff. Add about one quarter of this egg white mixture to the yolk mixture and whisk. Then add the ground almonds and breadcrumbs and carefully fold in the remaining egg white mixture.

Pour this mixture into prepared forms and place in a water bath. Bake at 325F/170C/Gas 3 for 35–40 minutes until firm. Test with a needle.

Turn out the puddings and serve with blood orange sauce, made by warming the orange juice and thickening with cornflour. Add segments and serve.

Chocolate Money Bags

L'Escargot, London
Chef Martin Lam

1 box filo pastry
1 lb. (450g.) bitter chocolate,
   grated coarsely
1 lb. (450g.) curd cheese
4 oz. (125g.) sultanas, soaked in
   2 fl. oz. (50ml.) dark rum
2 oz. (50g.) brown Barbados
   sugar
4 oz. (125g.) melted butter
3 egg yolks
½ pint (275ml.) double cream

Combine the cheese, sugar and egg yolks. Stir in the sultanas and rum and then ¾ lb. (350g.) of the grated chocolate.

Lay 3 sheets of filo pastry on a table dusted with icing sugar. Cut into 4 equal smaller squares. Put a dessert-spoonful of the mixture onto each square and then gather up the outsides to form the money bag. Refrigerate for 30 minutes and then drizzle with the melted butter and dust with icing sugar. Bake at 375F/190C/Gas 5 for 15 minutes.

Serve either hot or cold with the hot chocolate sauce made by melting the remaining chocolate with the cream until smooth – add some rum to flavour.

Oeufs à la Neige au Chocolat

Peacock Vane, Isle of Wight
Chef Rosalind Wolfenden

For the custard:

1 pint (570 ml.) whipping cream
6 oz. (175 g.) dark chocolate
7 egg yolks
2 tablespoons sugar

For the oeufs:

6 egg whites
12 oz. (350g.) caster sugar
milk for poaching
Praline or toasted flaked
    almonds, to decorate

Melt the chocolate and cream in the bain-marie. Beat the egg yolks with the sugar, and add to the chocolate cream. Stir gently over heat until required consistency is reached, (this shouldn't be too thick). Pour into a flat serving dish.

Beat the egg whites until very stiff and fold in sugar as for normal meringues.

Poach spoonfuls of meringue mixture in warm milk, (10–15 minutes each side), and slide into the chocolate custard.

To decorate, sprinkle with the praline of toasted flaked almonds. Serve warm or cold.

Cold

Mousse au Chocolat Amer

Buckland Manor, Buckland
Chef Martyn Pearn

Serves 4

6 oz. (175g.) bitter chocolate
  (Bourneville)
3 egg yolks
4 oz. (125g.) sugar
½ pint (275ml.) double cream
3½ fl. oz. (100ml.) armagnac

Melt the chocolate in a bain-marie, add the armagnac, egg yolks and sugar. Allow to cool.

Add the whipped cream.

Whip the egg whites to peaks, then add to the chocolate mixture. Pour into tall glasses and chill in the refrigerator.

Brown and White Chocolate Mousse

Country Garden, Ashburton
Chef/proprietor Hassan El-Masri

Serves 8

12 oz. (350g.) dark chocolate
12 oz. (350g.) white chocolate
1 oz. (25g.) butter
1 tablespoon Cointreau
1 tablespoon cognac
6 large eggs
blanched orange zest, to
    decorate

Melt the dark chocolate over a bain-marie with 3 tablespoons of water.

When melted add the butter with 3 egg yolks and Cointreau, whisk well. Remove from heat and fold in 3 stiffly beaten egg whites.

Pour this mixture into suitable glasses and allow to set for 2 hours. Repeat the process with the white chocolate and the remaining ingredients and pour this onto the set dark chocolate and decorate with blanched orange zest. Allow to set in the fridge.

Bitter Chocolate Mousse with Pineapple

Poole Court, Poole-in-Wharfedale
Chef Melvin Jordan

For the meringue:

3 egg whites
6 oz. (175g.) caster sugar

For the mousse:

1 small pineapple
10 oz. (275g.) bitter chocolate
3 egg yolks
3 egg whites
½ pint (275ml.) whipping cream
1 leaf gelatine
2 sheets of greaseproof paper

For the sauce:

pineapple trimmings
a little rum and sugar

This really is a most attractive sweet, with complementing flavours and a visually stunning presentation.

For the meringue, pre-set your oven to the lowest possible setting. Beat the egg whites until stiff and whisk in 4 oz. (125g.) of the sugar and then fold in the remaining 2 oz. (50g.). Line a flat baking sheet with greaseproof paper and with a metal ring approximately 2″ (2.5cm.) in diameter or perhaps using a jam jar, draw circles onto the paper. This will be the size guide for the meringue. Pipe the meringue onto the circle until they resemble a mushroom cap. Place in the oven and dry out without colouring for approximately 4 hours.

To prepare the pineapple and the mousse, cut the skin from the pineapple and slice the flesh about ½″ (1cm.) thick. Trim the slices to the same size as the meringue circles. Remove excess moisture from the pineapple by dabbing with kitchen paper. Set out carefully on a tray. Cut strips of greaseproof paper approximately 12″ (30.5cm.) long x 2½″ (6cm.) wide. Wrap these around the pineapple as you would do for a soufflé and staple or sellotape together at the join.

For the mousse, cut the chocolate into small pieces and place into a bowl. Separate the egg yolks from the white and whisk the whites into a peak. Soak the gelatine. Whisk the cream to soft peaks. Melt the chocolate in a bowl over a pan of simmering water. Remove and gently mix in the egg yolks and gelatine. Fold in the cream, then the egg whites and mix until smooth and combined. (N.B., the mixing of the mousse must be done as quickly as possible to avoid it setting too quickly). Pour into lined pineapple discs to a depth of approximately 1½" (3.5cm.). Allow to set in fridge. When set, remove the greaseproof and top with a meringue shell.

For the sauce, put the pineapple trimmings in a pan. Add a little water, rum and sugar and bring to the boil. Simmer for a couple of minutes and leave. Liquidise and serve a small amount of chilled sauce on each plate.

Chocolate and Hazelnut Mousse

Marlfield House, Gorey
Chef Tom Galvin

½ pint (275ml.) milk
2 oz. (50g.) caster sugar
5 fl. oz. (150ml.) cream
2 eggs
4 leaves gelatine
2 oz. (50g.) chocolate
   couverture
2 oz. (50g.) hazelnuts, chopped

Soak the gelatine in cold water.

Cream the yolks and sugar in a bowl until almost white.

Bring the milk to the boil and dissolve the chocolate in it. Whisk the milk and chocolate mixture into the yolks and sugar, mixing well. Return to a low heat and stir continuously with a wooden spoon until the mixture coats the back of the spoon. The mixture must not boil.

Remove from the heat, add the gelatine and stir until dissolved. Place in a clean bowl and leave to cool, stirring occasionally until almost setting point.

When almost set fold in the lightly beaten cream, then the stiffly beaten egg whites and finally the chopped hazelnuts. Refrigerate.

Mousse of Chocolate with Mint Cream

Royal Crescent Hotel, Bath
Chef Michael Croft

Serves 6

1 pint (570ml.) crème Anglaise
  (English custard)
3 leaves gelatine
8 oz. (225g.) white couverture
  chocolate
green Chartreuse
green colouring
16 fl. oz. (450ml.) cream, lightly
  whipped

In 2 bowls over simmering water separately melt the dark and the white chocolate.

Make the crème Anglaise in the traditional manner.

Melt the gelatine in the warm crème Anglaise. Pass through a sieve and then split into 2 bowls. Add the dark melted chocolate to one and the white melted chocolate to the other.

Cool and fold in half the whipped cream to the dark mousse and pour into 6 caramel moulds. Set in the fridge.

Remove moulds from the fridge and scoop out the centres with an ice cream scoop. Fill with the white mousse mixture to which has been added green Chartreuse colouring. Set in the fridge.

To serve, demould and scoop out a corner of the mousse to expose the green centre. Place the scooped piece on the plate and pour a cordon of pale green cream flavoured with Chartreuse around the mousse.

Light Chocolate and Banana Mousse

Bowlish House, Shepton Mallet
Proprietors Julia and Brian Jordan

Serves 6

8 oz. (225g.) white chocolate
2 egg yolks
2 oz. (50g.) caster sugar
2 leaves of gelatine
½ pint (275ml.) milk
5 fl. oz. (150ml.) double cream
2 bananas
lemon juice
cooking brandy

The affect of this excellent dish is enhanced and the layering is easier if the banana is sliced in long diagonals rather than simply chopped through. As an alternative you could either use tinned manderins or oranges which have had all the pith removed, and orange chocolate.

Slice the bananas and immerse in the lemon juice and the brandy.

Whisk the egg yolks and sugar until nearly white in colour.

Soften the gelatine leaves in cold water.

Boil the milk and gently pour onto the egg and sugar mixture. Pour this mixture back into the milk pan and return to a low heat stirring continuously until the mixture thickens – do not allow to boil.

After thickening, remove from the heat and add the chocolate which has been softened or melted separately and the softened gelatine leaves. The whole mixture will blend itself together with the residual heat from the milk. Leave until cool.

Pass through a sieve and add the double cream which has been softly whipped.

Line a glass terrine or bowl with clingfilm and pour in a little of the liquid mixture. Add a layer of banana slices and another layer of the mixture until the ingredients have been used up. Leave to set firm in a refrigerator.

To serve, upend the terrine or bowl onto a sufficiently large plate and carefully remove the cling film which will adhere to the chocolate.

Rich Chocolate Mousse with Coffee Sauce

Billesley Manor, Billesley
Chef Michael Monahan

Serves 10

1 lb. (450g.) bitter chocolate
3 tablespoons milk
3 tablespoons cream
3 oz. (75g.) icing sugar
8 eggs
3 fl. oz. (75ml.) rum

For the sauce:

½ pint (275ml.) milk
½ pint (275ml.) cream
3 oz. (75g.) sugar
4 egg yolks
1 oz. (25g.) coffee (instant)
coffee flavoured cream
white chocolate, melted for
   decoration

To make the chocolate mousse, first melt the chocolate with milk and cream.

Add the icing sugar and rum. Cool slightly and whisk in the egg yolks. Leave to stand for a few minutes and gently fold in the stiffly beaten egg whites. Pour into a glass bowl and refrigerate.

To make the sauce, bring the milk to the boil with the coffee. Place the sugar and egg yolks in a basin and whisk together for 5 minutes. Add the coffee milk to the eggs and sugar whisking quickly so as not to curdle the eggs. Return the mixture to a pan and heat gently until it thickens and coats the back of a spoon. Do not allow the sauce to boil. Strain and cool.

To serve take a cold dessert plate and spoon some of the coffee sauce on. Pipe a rosette of coffee flavoured cream in the middle and arrange 3 quenelles of chocolate mousse around the cream. Place a white chocolate runount on top of the coffee cream for decoration.

White Chocolate Mousse with Dark Chocolate Sauce

Partners 23, Sutton
Chef/proprietor Tim McEntire

For the mousse:

4 oz. (125g.) white chocolate
3 oz. (75g.) sugar
2 fl. oz. (50ml.) milk
1 leaf gelatine
14 fl. oz. (400ml.) whipping
   cream

For the sauce:

3 oz. (75g.) dark chocolate
5 fl. oz. (150ml.) milk
½ oz. (15g.) sugar
1 egg yolk

praline roughly chopped to
   decorate

To make the mousse, soak the gelatine in cold water. Gently melt the white chocolate in a bowl over simmering water. Dissolve the sugar in warm milk, add the gelatine and beat vigorously into the melted chocolate. Strain. Lightly whip the cream and fold into the chocolate mixture, place into individual moulds.

To make the dark sauce, gently melt the chocolate in a bowl over simmering water. Boil the milk and sugar together, pour onto the egg yolk, whisking all the time. Add to the melted chocolate and cool.

To serve, unmould the mousse and place in the centre of the plate. Robe each mousse with dark sauce. Decorate with a little roughly chopped praline.

Chilled Chocolate Curd Pudding with Apricots and Almonds

Restaurant Roger Burdell, Loughborough
Chef/proprietor Roger Burdell

Serves 6

1 measure of apricot liqueur
8 oz. (225g.) chocolate
  couverture
1 fl. oz. (25ml.) milk
4 egg yolks
2 oz. (50g.) caster sugar
3 fl. oz. (75ml.) milk
5 oz. (150g.) curds
5 fl. oz. (150ml.) curds
5 fl. oz. (150ml.) whipping
  cream
2oz. (50g.) flaked almonds,
  toasted
1–2 lbs. (450–900g.) apricots,
  poached and chilled

Melt the first three items together gently.

Whisk the next three items together over steam until the mixture has thickened.

Whip the cream and then beat the curds into it, which should be medium dry yet smooth.

Combine the chocolate mixture with the egg yolk mousse and allow to cool a little. Fold in the curd mixture and the almonds. Spoon into moulds or ramekins and chill overnight. Serve with poached apricots and more toasted almonds.

Chocolate Dolce

Popjoys, Bath
Chef/proprietor Ali Golden

Serves 12

few tablespoons Amaretto or
the liqueur of your choice
9 oz. (250g.) good plain
chocolate (Menier)
1 lb. (450g.) unsalted butter
9 eggs, separated
12 oz. (350g.) caster sugar
15 oz. (425g.) plain biscuits
(Rich Tea or Nice), roughly
crushed NOT crumbs
double cream for decoration

Melt the chocolate and butter in a bain-marie. Add the liqueur.

Beat the egg yolks and sugar until pale. Stir the crushed biscuits into the egg mixture and gradually stir in the melted butter and chocolate. Mix well together. Cool the mixture slightly.

Whisk the egg whites until peaky and fold gently into the chocolate mixture with a metal spoon. Spoon into little dishes and chill for 8 hours or overnight. Decorate with whipped cream to which a little liqueur of your choice has been added.

Chocolate Palobo

Peacock Vane, Isle of Wight
Chef Rosalind Wolfenden

12 oz. (350g.) plain dessert
   chocolate
6 eggs
4–5 oz. (125–150g.) caster
   sugar
4 oz. (125g.) butter

This very rich chocolate mousse, which has been part of the Peacock Vane's repertoire for at least the last twenty years, was given to Mrs Joan Wolfenden by her Spanish staff in the 1960's, and was said to have come from Spanish South America. I have always presumed that Palobo is a contraction of the Spanish 'Para el lobo', 'for the wolf'.

Separate the egg. Whisk the yolks and sugar until light and pale in colour.

Melt the chocolate with butter in a bain-marie, and allow to cool a little.

Whisk the egg white until stiff. Beat chocolate and butter into yolks and sugar, and then fold in egg whites.

Pour into a glass dish and refrigerate. Palobo is always better the next day!

Chocolate Pots with Preserved Orange Peel

Morels, Haslemere
Chef/proprietor J. Morel

Serves 6–8

7 oz. (200g.) bitter chocolate,
  broken into small pieces
11 fl. oz. (300ml.) single cream
1 egg
3½ oz. (100g.) preserved
  orange peel

Bring the cream to the boil and add the chocolate.
Liquidise, adding the whole egg.

Chop the preserved orange peel into small pieces and add
to the mixture. Pour into ramekins and cook gently in a
bain-marie for 15–20 minutes. Leave to cool, chill and serve.

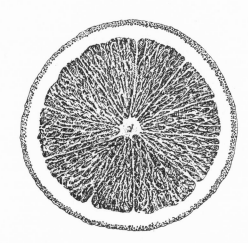

Chocolate Saint Emilion

The Wife of Bath, Wye
Chef/proprietor Bob Johnson

1 packet ratafias
2 tablespoons brandy
6 oz. (175g.) dark chocolate
½ pint (275ml.) double cream
4 eggs, separated
2 oz. (50g.) butter

Soak the ratafias in the brandy.

Melt the chocolate and butter in a double saucepan until smooth. Beat in the egg yolks and allow to cool a little. Whisk the egg whites and cream and fold together.

Place a layer of brandy soaked ratafias in the bottom of each ramekin and cover with the chocolate mixture. Refrigerate for 2 hours before serving.

Crème Velour

Bowlish House, Shepton Mallet
Proprietors Julia and Brian Jordan

Serves 6

2½ oz. (60g.) good dark
   chocolate
6 oz. (175g.) cream cheese
1½ oz. (40g.) caster sugar
½ pint (275ml.) double cream
1 tablespoon brandy

Soften the cream cheese. Add the sugar and whisk until smooth.

Melt the chocolate with a few drops of water in a bowl over a simmering pan half full of water. Add the melted chocolate to the cream cheese and whisk so that the mixture remains smooth.

Lightly whip the cream and fold into the cheese and chocolate mixture. Flavour with the brandy and give a final whisk until the mixture forms soft peaks. Put into serving dishes or glasses and serve chilled.

Petit Pot Au Chocolat

Hilaire, London
Chef/proprietor Simon Hopkinson

Serves 8 (generously)

1 lb. (450g.) chocolate
1 pint (570 ml.) double cream
½ pint (275ml.) milk
1 split vanilla pod
5 egg yolks
3½ oz. (100g.) icing sugar

These will keep well for about 1 week covered with cling film.

Melt together slowly in a pan over boiling water the first four ingredients until perfectly smooth. Discard the vanilla pod.

Meanwhile beat together the egg yolks and sugar. Pour them onto the chocolate mixture blending together very thoroughly.

Pour into individual ramekins and bake in a bain-marie at 350F/180C/Gas 4 for approximately 40 minutes until lightly puffed up and shiny. Cool thoroughly and leave in the refrigerator until very cold.

Serve alone. Eating this with cream could do serious damage to your arteries . . . !!

Rum Chocolate Truffle

Fox & Goose, Fressingfield
Chef/proprietor A. P. Clarke

8 eggs, separated
½ lb. (225g.) plain chocolate
5 oz. (150g.) butter, cut into
    small cubes
7½ fl. oz. (215ml.) rum
7½ fl. oz. (215ml.) whipped
    cream to decorate
freshly toasted almonds to
    decorate

Melt the chocolate in a bowl over simmering water. When the chocolate has completely melted gently stir in the butter. Add the egg yolks, and then add the rum. You should now have a fairly thick chocolate mixture.

Beat the egg whites until very firm. Gently fold the chocolate mixture into the egg whites until completely incorporated. Now place the truffle mixture into ramekin dishes and refrigerate for at least 24 hours.

Decorate the individual truffles with whipped cream and freshly toasted almonds.

White Chocolate Truffle with Praline and Dark Chocolate Sauce

Rogers, Windermere
Chef/proprietor Roger Pergl-Wilson

Serves 4

5 oz. (150ml.) white chocolate
½ pint (275ml.) double cream
1 oz. (25g.) sugar
1 oz. (25g.) flaked almonds

For the sauce (it is best to make this sauce the day before):

1 oz. (25g.) cocoa powder
2 oz. (50g.) caster sugar
1 tablespoon golden syrup
½ teaspoon instant coffee
slightly less than 5 fl. oz.
   (150ml.) water
1 teaspoon unsalted butter

Melt the chocolate and leave to cool.

Make the praline by toasting the almonds in the oven till golden brown. Cook the sugar to caramel and add the warm almonds. Pour out onto a lightly oiled surface. When cold crush with a rolling pin.

Whip the cream halfway towards firmness. Fold in the cool chocolate and the praline, reserving a little for garnish. Pour into ramekins that have been lightly oiled and chill well in a fridge.

To make the sauce, sieve the cocoa powder, and mix with the sugar and coffee. Whisk in the water until a smooth cream. Bring gently to the boil stirring all the while. Add the butter and mix well in. Leave to cool and then refrigerate.

Turn out truffle and surround with sauce. Top with cream and praline and decorate with mint or chocolate leaf.

Marquise au Chocolat Blanc

Capital Hotel, London
Chef Brian Turner

Serves 8

2 fl. oz. (50ml.) water
1 oz. (25g.) glucose
pinch salt
2 leaves gelatine, soaked
3 egg yolks
18 fl. oz. (500ml.) whipped
   cream, cooled
9 oz. (250g.) couverture
   chocolate, chopped
sponge fingers, 2 per person
sponge

Bring the water and the glucose to the boil. Add the gelatine and chocolate. Remove from heat and beat out any lumps. Allow to cool.

When cool, add the egg yolks and fold in the cream. Fill a 1 lb. (45g.) loaf tin with the mixture and cover with sponge. Place in a chiller and leave for 24 hours.

To serve, slightly warm the outside of the tin in hot water and turn out. Slice and serve on a plate, on chocolate sauce, accompanied with sponge fingers.

Marquise aux Deux Chocolats

Le Poulbot, London
Chef Rowley Leigh

For the biscuit:

11 oz. (300g.) blanched
  almonds
7 oz. (200g.) roasted and
  peeled hazelnuts
4 tablespoons plain flour
8 egg whites, stiffly beaten
9 oz. (250g.) caster sugar

For the dark ganache:

18 oz. (500g.) best quality
  couverture chocolate
18 oz. (500g.) double cream,
  lightly whipped

For the white ganache:

11 oz. (300g.) white chocolate
7 fl. oz. (200ml.) double cream,
  lightly whipped
3 oz. (75g.) pistachio nuts
Café Anglaise

For the biscuit, roast the nuts and leave to cool. Chop finely. Mix the nuts with the flour and the sugar and fold into the stiffly beaten egg whites. Spread onto a buttered and floured tray and cook in a medium oven. When set, cut into 4 long strips and replace in the oven to dry out at a very low temperature.

For the dark ganache, melt the chocolate in a bowl over simmering water to blood temperature and fold in the lightly whipped cream.

For the white ganache, blanch, peel and lightly chop the pistachios. Melt the white chocolate in a bowl over simmering water to blood temperature and fold into the lightly whipped cream. Fold the nuts into the chocolate mixture.

Assemble the marquise on a board in layers. First a length of biscuit, then some white ganache, then biscuit then dark ganache, biscuit, white ganache, biscuit, and then mask the whole with dark ganache. Place in fridge to set.

Serve with a sauce Café Anglaise (a light custard, flavoured with roasted coffee beans).

Marquise of Two Chocolates with Almond and Hazelnut Meringue

Gidleigh Park, Chagford
Chef Shaun Hill

Serves 4–6

6 oz. (175g.) dark chocolate
1 fl. oz. (25ml.) coffee
3 oz. (75g.) butter

For the white chocolate:

3 oz. (75g.) white chocolate
drop vanilla essence
2 tablespoons milk
2 egg yolks
4 oz. (125g.) caster sugar
½ oz. (5g.) gelatine dissolved in
  6 tablespoons water
5 fl. oz. (150ml.) double cream
5 fl. oz. (150ml.) soured cream

For the meringue:

4 oz. (125g.) almonds and
  hazelnuts, blanched
1 tablespoon plain flour
3 egg whites

For the white chocolate, place the milk in a saucepan with the vanilla and white chocolate and melt gently. Whisk the egg yolks and sugar. When the chocolate is completely melted add it to the egg/sugar mixture. Cook over a gentle heat, whisking continuously until the mixture thickens – take care not to boil. Add 2 tablespoons of gelatine and allow to cool. Beat the cream and soured cream together until firm. Add half to the white chocolate mixture and refrigerate.

Make the meringue by grinding together the nuts and mixing together with the flour and 2 oz. (50g.) of caster sugar. Whisk the egg whites till firm and then fold into the nut mixture. Spread onto a 6 x 3" (15 x 7.5cm.) baking tray lined with Bakewell paper. Bake for 12 minutes as 400F/200C/Gas 6. Leave to cool.

Place the dark chocolate in a saucepan with the coffee and the remaining sugar. Heat gently till melted. Add the butter, stir well, add the remaining gelatine and allow to cool. When cool add the remaining cream.

To assemble, line a 10 x 3" (25 x 7.5cm.) cake tin with Bakewell paper. Pour in half the dark chocolate mixture. Cut the meringue into two rectangles and place one on top of the chocolate mixture. Spread the white chocolate mixture on top of the meringue. Place the second rectangle of meringue on top of the white chocolate cream. Pour over the rest of the dark chocolate cream and allow 24 hours to set.

Chocolate Terrine

Pool Court, Pool-in-Wharfedale
Chef Melvin Jordan

For the white mousse:

1 egg yolk
2 oz. (50g.) Milky Bar, grated
2 fl. oz. (50ml.) milk
1 sheet soaked leaf gelatine
2 tablespoons kirsch
1 dessertspoon caster sugar
½ pint (275ml.) whipped cream

For the milk mousse:

1 egg yolk
2 oz. (50g.) milk chocolate,
   grated
2 fl. oz. (50ml.) milk
1 sheet soaked leaf gelatine
1 dessertspoon caster sugar
½ pint (275ml.) whipped cream

This recipe is not as complicated as it seems because the methods for all the above mousses are the same. The recipe does not work very well if made in small quantities, but the terrine will keep for two to three days.

Make all the mousses separately. In a pan put the egg yolk, milk, sugar and spirit and stir over a low heat until it coats the back of a spoon. Do not boil as this will curdle the milk. Take off the heat and add the chocolate. Stir until melted and then add the soaked gelatine. Keep all the mousses in a warm place till the whipped cream is added.

Whip the cream into soft peaks and fold into each mousse mixture. When all are mixed layer a mould until filled. Cover with greaseproof paper. Place in fridge to set for 5 hours.

For the plain chocolate mousse:

1 egg yolk
2 oz. (50g.) Bourneville, grated
2 fl. oz. (50ml.) milk
1 sheet soaked leaf gelatine
2 dessertspoons rum
1 dessertspoon caster sugar
½ pint (275ml.) whipped cream

To turn out, run the base of the terrine under hot water and tip out onto a board. Keep refrigerated till ready to serve. Serve with an almond sauce, made by whipping ½ pint (275ml.) of cream until it becomes thick. Fold in 2 dessertspoons of caster sugar, 1 oz. (25g.) ground almonds and a drop of almond essence. Garnish the sauce with toasted almonds and perhaps some fresh strawberries.

Chocolate and Pear Terrine

Royal Crescent Hotel, Bath
Chef Michael Croft

Serves 12

2 small pears, peeled and
  cored and cooked in a stock
  syrup
1 flat chocolate genoise
  sponge (as for swiss roll)

For the mousse:

8 oz. (225g.) dark couverture
  chocolate
2 leaves gelatine
3½ fl. oz. (100ml.) Poire William
  liqueur
20 fl. oz. (1 litre) cream

For the sauce:

2 egg yolks
1 oz. (25g.) sugar
½ pint (275ml.) milk
Crème de Menthe

Line a terrine mould with neatly cut pieces of sponge so that it is evenly covered.

Melt the chocolate over a gentle heat and add the gelatine and the liqueur. When just melted and no visible lumps appear remove from heat and cool gently.

Fold in the whipped cream and spoon immediately into the mould until half full. Place pieces of poached pear through the terrine and cover with mousse. Finally place another piece of sponge on top and set in the fridge.

For the sauce, mix 2 egg yolks to 1 oz. (25g.) sugar and add the boiling milk and return to the pan. Gently bring back to the heat until the mixture slightly thickens – do not boil. Allow to cool and flavour with Crème de Menthe.

Turn the terrine out of its mould onto a wooden board and cut a thin slice. Place onto a plate surrounding it with pale green mint sauce.

50

Delice au Chocolat

La Ciboulette, Cheltenham
Chef/proprietor Kevin Jenkins

Serves 6–8

For the sponge:

2 eggs
1 oz. (25g.) cocoa
1 oz. (25g.) flour
14 oz. (400g.) Bourneville
15 fl. oz. (425ml.) double cream
1 oz. (25g.) cocoa powder
fresh custard, flavoured with
  Drambuie

Make the chocolate sponge and use as a base for a flan ring.

Melt the chocolate in a bowl over simmering water. Gently fold in the slightly whipped cream and pour onto the base. Set in the fridge for 1 hour. Sprinkle with cocoa powder and serve with a fresh custard flavoured with Drambuie.

Delice de Chocolat aux Bananes

French Partridge, Horton
Chef/proprietor David Partridge

Serves 6

Bananas, sliced

For the sponge:

2 oz. (50g.) caster sugar
¾ oz. (20g.) cocoa
2 eggs, separated
1 teaspoon water

For the mousse:

3 oz. (75g.) good quality plain
chocolate
5 fl. oz. (150ml.) double cream,
lightly whipped

Make the chocolate mousse by melting the chocolate in a bowl over simmering water. Cool and stir into the lightly whipped cream. Cool.

Whisk the yolks with the water, sugar and cocoa mixture. Fold in the stiffly beaten egg whites.

Oil a non-stick baking tray and spoon onto it circles of the mixture approximately 5" (12.5cm.) in diameter. Bake in a moderate oven for about 5 minutes until the sponge is set.

Remove from the tray very carefully and allow to cool before filling with the chocolate mousse and sliced bananas. Fold over, omelette fashion and pipe whipped cream along the open edges.

Bowlish Zucotto

Bowlish House, Shepton Mallet
Proprietors Julia and Brian Jordan

Serves 6

½ pint (275ml.) double cream
¾ oz. (15g.) icing sugar
1 oz. (25g.) toasted hazelnuts
4 oz. (125g.) stoned black
  cherries
2 oz. (50g.) dark plain
  chocolate, grated
2 tablespoons brandy
2 tablespoons orange juice

This dish is usually put into a large, steep sided, glass bowl lined with boudoir biscuits soaked in brandy. We find it easier to make and to use by only using the filling of the dish.

Whip the cream and the icing sugar together until fairly stiff.

Crush the hazelnuts and slice the cherries into small pieces and add to the cream and sugar mix. Fold in the grated chocolate.

Stir in the orange juice and the brandy.

Put the mixture into reasonable sized wine glasses or small glass bowls and chill before serving.

Chocolate Box filled with Almond Cream and Poached Apricots, with Apricot Purée

Restaurant Seventy Four, Canterbury
Chef/proprietor I. L. Mcandrew

Serves 4

8 oz. (225g.) dark chocolate
2 lbs. (900g.) small apricots
5 fl. oz. (500ml.) double cream
1 oz. (25g.) icing sugar
amaretto to taste
½ pint (275ml.) sugar syrup
2 oz. (50g.) ground almonds,
   browned in oven or under grill
   and toasted
½ lemon

Using cotton wool, polish the insides of four oval or square moulds, approximately 3 x 2 x 1½" (7.5 x 5 x 4 cm.), to prevent the chocolate from sticking.

Cut the chocolate into small pieces and melt in a bowl over hot water. Do not allow the chocolate above blood heat. Using a clean dry brush, coat the inside of the moulds with a thin layer of melted chocolate and allow to set. Once set pour the chocolate into each mould, one at a time filling them up and then tipping the chocolate out again. This will leave a thin layer of chocolate. Allow these to set in the refrigerator for at least half an hour.

To make the lids, cover the back of a small tray on a board with clingfilm, and spread a thin layer of chocolate onto this. when it is almost set mark out four lids by placing a mould of the same size on the chocolate and cutting round. Leave to set in a refrigerator.

Put four good apricots to one side and cut the rest into eights. Poach these in the sugar syrup until soft. Drain from the syrup, saving about 40 pieces (for filling the box). Place the rest into a food blender or processor with the juice of half a lemon and whizz until a smooth purée. Rub this purée through a sieve. This is the sauce, if you fear it is little too thick thin it down with some of the cooking liquor.

Poach the four reserved apricots in the syrup until they are just cooked. Allow to cool and remove skins.

Gently remove the boxes from their moulds, and half fill each one with the almond cream. Fill the rest of the box with pieces of apricot, and place a dab of cream on one edge of each box and finish by placing a lid on by using the cream by holding it at an angle.

To serve place the box slightly off centre of each plate, pour a spoonful of the sauce onto the plate next to the box and place a whole apricot or mint leaf to the side of both the box and the sauce.

Chocolate Eggs with a Coffee Cream Sauce

Rogers, Windermere
Chef/proprietor Roger Pergl-Wilson

Serves 4

3 egg whites
1 oz. (25g.) caster sugar
1 dessertspoon sieved cocoa
powder
2 pints (generous litre) water
2 oz. (50g.) sugar, for poaching

For the sauce:

7 fl. oz. (200ml.) double cream
1 egg yolk
1 oz. (25g.) caster sugar
1 tablespoon freshly ground
coffee

To make the sauce, bring the cream to the boil and turn off the heat. Allow to rest for a minute and add the coffee. Cover and allow to infuse. Beat the egg yolk and sugar together and sieve the coffee cream through a fine sieve onto the egg and sugar mix. Whisk well. Return to the heat and stir gently till just below boiling point. Do not re-boil. Remove from heat and cool. Refrigerate.

For the eggs, whisk the whites till firm. Mix the sugar and cocoa together and fold into the whites. Bring the water and sugar to the boil and keep just below simmering. Using two tablespoons shape the meringue into eggs and poach lightly for 30 seconds turning gently. Lift out onto a plate. Make 8 eggs and cool.

To serve pour the sauce onto individual serving plates. Dust the eggs lightly with cocoa powder and place two eggs on each plate. Run a thread of cream through the coffee sauce. Garnish with a chocolate leaf.

Chocolate Meringue Nests with Fresh Cherries and Maraschino

Marlfield House, Gorey
Chef Tom Galvin

Serves 4–6

4 oz. (125g.) chocolate
 couverture
½ pint (275ml.) double cream,
 stiffly whipped
½ pint (275ml.) maraschino
1 punnet cherries, stoned

For the meringues:

4 egg whites
8 oz. (225g.) caster sugar

Make the meringues by whipping the egg whites stiffly. Sprinkle on the sugar and carefully mix in. Place into a piping bag with a plain tube and pipe onto a greaseproofed tray in the shape of nests. Bake in a slow oven.

In a bowl, over simmering water, gently melt the chocolate. Dip the meringues into the melted chocolate and coat.

Mix together the stiffly whipped cream with the maraschino. Fold in the cherries reserving 7–8 for decoration. Place the cream mixture into the chocolate meringues.

Chocolate and Mint Bavarois with Fresh Mint Sauce

Sharrow Bay, Ullswater
Chef Alison Kennedy

Serves 4

For the mint bavarois:

5 fl. oz. (150ml.) milk
2 egg yolks
2 oz. (50g.) caster sugar
1 teaspoon gelatine dissolved
  in a little water
5 fl. oz. (150ml.) double cream
peppermint oil to taste

For the chocolate bavarois:

½ pint (275ml.) milk
2 oz. (50g.) chocolate
2 oz. (50g.) sugar
2 egg yolks
¼ oz. (5g.) gelatine dissolved in
  a little water
5 fl. oz. (150ml.) double cream

For the mint sauce:

½ pint (275ml.) milk
handful of fresh mint
3 egg yolks and 3 oz. (75g.)
  sugar, mixed together

Make the mint bavarois by bringing the milk to the boil and remove from the heat. Cream the egg yolks and sugar to the ribbon stage. Pour on the milk and return to the pan and thicken without boiling. Strain into a bowl. Dissolve the gelatine over a gentle heat. When melted add to the custard and allow to cool. Fold in the whipped cream and flavour with peppermint oil.

Make the chocolate bavarois by melting the chocolate with the milk and then proceeding as with the mint bavarois.

Layer the two bavarois in one large dish or small ramekins and serve with the mint sauce.

Make the mint sauce by boiling the milk and mint together. Pour onto the mixture of egg and sugar and return to the pan. Cook until thick and strain into a jug and cool.

Chocolate Pancakes Filled with Crème de Menthe Cream

Corse Lawn House, Corse Lawn
Chef/proprietor Baba Hine

For the pancakes:

4 eggs
4 tablespoons flour
15 fl. oz. (400ml.) milk
2 tablespoons chocolate
   powder
2 tablespoons rum
1 tablespoon melted butter
1 tablespoon sugar

For the cream:

1 pint (570ml.) double cream
6 tablespoons Crème de
   Menthe
3 tablespoons sugar

Beat all the pancake ingredients together and proceed with the pancakes in the usual way. Allow to cool.

Whip the cream till very stiff and fold in the Crème de Menthe and sugar.

Fill the pancakes with the cream and decorate with more cream piped in star shapes.

Chocolate Roulade

Bowlish House, Shepton Mallet
Proprietors Julia and Brian Jordan

Serves 6

6 oz. (175g.) dark plain
   chocolate
5 eggs
8 oz. (225g.) caster sugar
3–4 tablespoons water
½ pint (275ml.) double cream
   for the filling
rum, brandy or vanilla essence
   for flavouring the cream
icing sugar for dusting

Separate the eggs and gradually beat the yolks into the caster sugar until lemon coloured.

Melt the chocolate in the bowl over simmering water.

Whip the egg whites until firm peaks will hold.

Add the chocolate to the egg yolk and sugar mixture and cut and fold the whipped egg whites into this.

Turn the mixture into a large baking tin lined with oiled greaseproof paper and bake in a pre-heated oven at 350F/180C/Gas 4 for 10 minutes. Remove and allow to cool slightly, then cover with a damp cloth and leave in the fridge or in a cool place over night – or for at least 12 hours.

Lay a sheet of fresh greaseproof paper, dusted with icing sugar, on top of the roulade and turn upside down so that the previous sheet can be removed. Spread the whole surface with the whipped cream into which you have added your flavouring. (Alternatively, finely chopped fresh summer fruit can be mixed with the whipping cream instead of the alcohol or vanilla essence).

Finally roll the sheet of roulade into a swiss roll using the undersheet of greaseproof paper to assist. Dust with icing sugar.

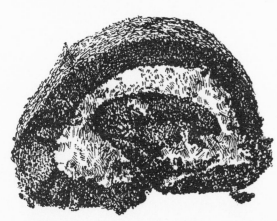

Chocolate Shell Cakes

Popjoys, Bath
Chef/proprietor Ali Golden

8 oz. (225g.) butter
6 oz. (175g.) plain chocolate
3 oz. (75g.) cocoa
6 oz. (175g.) plain flour
6 eggs
6 oz. (175g.) caster sugar
6 scallop shells
chocolate mousse or coffee
  cream
cake gold-leaf to decorate
  (available from specialist
  kitchen shops)

Grease the scallop shells with butter.

Melt chocolate and the butter together.

Sift the cocoa and flour together.

Beat the eggs and sugar until pale and moussey.

Fold together gently, first the chocolate and then the sifted mixture. Line the scallop shells with the mixture and bake in oven at 180F/350C/gas 4 for 20–25 minutes. Turn out onto a rack to cool.

Split the chocolate shell cases from the scallop shells and fill with chocolate mousse or coffee cream piped in squiggles from a star shaped nozzle. Either dredge with caster sugar or paint with cake gold-leaf for a dramatic effect.

Feuilleté de Chocolat aux Framboises

Restaurant Bosquet, Kenilworth
Chef/proprietor Bernard Lignier

Serves 8–10

For the chocolate puff pastry:

1 lb. (450g.) strong plain white
flour
2 oz. (50g.) cocoa powder
3½ oz. (100g.) butter (plus 18
oz.–500g. butter)
12 fl. oz. (350ml.) water

For the filling:

18 fl. oz. (500ml.) double cream
22 oz. (600g.) fresh raspberries
10 passion fruits, juiced
icing sugar
caster sugar

Make the puff pastry in the classical way, by mixing the ingredients, except for the larger amount of butter, resting for 2 hours and then adding the butter and giving 6 folds.

Spread the pastry ¾" (2cm.) thick on an oven tray and cook in oven at 450F/230C/Gas 8 for 10 minutes – then for a further 8 minutes at 350F/180C/Gas 4, with another tray on top to keep it flat. Cool and cut into desired shape.

Sugar the passion fruit juice to taste and whip with the double cream. Sieve 5 oz. (150g.) of the raspberries to make a coulis. Put a drop of the passion fruit cream on a plate so that the first layer of pastry does not slip. Place cream and raspberries on top of the pastry and then top with another layer of pastry. Dust with icing sugar and decorate with raspberries and mint leaves. Pour the raspberry coulis around the plate.

Fondant au Chocolat et Kumquats

Restaurant Bosquet, Kenilworth
Chef/proprietor Bernard Lignier

Serves 12–15

For the fondant:

18 oz. (500g.) dark bitter
   chocolate
2 lb. (scant kilo) kumquats
1 pint (570ml.) double cream
1½ lb. (750g.) granulated sugar

For the sauce:

3½ oz. (100g.) chocolate
Grand Marnier
juice 2 oranges
syrup left over from cooking
   kumquats

Boil the sugar with 1 pint (570ml.) of water and simmer the kumquats for 3 hours, slowly.

Break the chocolate into little pieces. Bring the cream to the boil, add the chocolate and cook for 2 minutes. Cool and whip before the mixture gets too stiff – whisk till light and fluffy.

Drain the kumquats and take out the pips and add to the chocolate mixture.

Line a terrine mould with cling film and fill up with the mixture. Cool in the fridge for at least 3 hours before serving. Make a sauce by melting the chocolate with the left over syrup, orange juice and Grand Marnier to taste.

Fondant de Chocolat aux Raisins

Longueville Manor, Jersey
Chef John Dicken

For the shortbread mix:

4 oz. (125g.) sultanas, soaked
　in 1 fl. oz. (25ml.) overnight
9 fl. oz. (250ml.) milk
3 oz. (75g.) sugar
5 egg yolks
9 oz. (250g.) milk chocolate
2 leaves gelatine, softened in
　cold water
9 fl. oz. (250ml.) cream
11 oz. (300g.) butter

Roll and line the base of an 8 x 2" (20.5 x 5cm.) flan ring with a sheet of shortbread and bake.

Boil the milk and slowly pour onto the egg yolks and sugar. Return to the pan and using a thermometer, and stirring well, increase until you reach 80C. Pass through a fine chinoise into a bowl.

Add the chopped chocolate into the egg yolk mixture (which is hot) and stir until dissolved. Add the softened gelatine and continue to add the butter. The mixture should be slowly setting – if not, help it along on a bowl of iced water. Gently fold in the lightly whipped cream.

Arrange the soaked sultanas on the shortbread and pour on the chocolate fondant, allow to set in the refrigerator. This is delicious when served with a light apple and lime coulis.

Brandied Chocolate Trifle

The White House, Williton
Chef/proprietor Kay Smith

For the sponge:

4 eggs, separated
6 oz. (175g.) caster sugar
1½ oz. (25g.) cocoa powder
equal quantities of rum/milk or
 brandy/milk to soak the
 sponge

Four the mousse ingredients:

4 fl. oz. (125ml.) strong black
 coffee
8 oz. (225g.) plain chocolate
4 eggs, separated
2 oz. (50g.) caster sugar

For the sponge, grease or line with silicone paper 2, 8″ (20.5cm.) flan dishes. Whisk the sugar and the yolks until light and creamy and double in bulk. Add the sieved cocoa powder, thoroughly amalgamating. Fold in the stiffly beaten whites. Divide the mixture into flan dishes and bake at 350F/180C/Gas 4 for 15 minutes, or until just cooked, but not too dry. Turn out. When cool cut the sponge in half horizontally and sprinkle with the brandy mix. Set aside.

For the mousse, gently melt the chocolate with the coffee in a heavy saucepan on a very low heat. Meanwhile whisk the yolks with the sugar until double in bulk. Mix in the melted chocolate and gently fold in stiffly beaten eggs.

To assemble, in a loose bottomed 8″ (20.5cm.) cake tin, lined with silicon paper, place a brandy soaked half of sponge and gently spread with quarter of the mousse mixture. Repeat this process eventually finishing with a layer of mousse. Chill until set. Remove from tin and serve with thick cream – delicious!!

Chestnut, Chocolate and Prune Pudding

Hope End, Ledbury
Chef/proprietor Patricia Hegarty

Serves 6

9 large Californian prunes,
   18–24 in size
6 oz. (175g.) dried chestnuts
vanilla pod
2 tablespoons honey
3 oz. (75g.) strong bitter
   chocolate
double cream to decorate

The day before, simmer the prunes in water for 10 minutes and leave to swell. Soak the chestnuts.

Next day cook the chestnuts and vanilla pod in ¾ pint (400ml.) of water until they will mash easily.

Drain, retaining the liquor, and process with the honey. The consistency should be fairly stiff. Correct with the reserved liquor if necessary.

Melt the chocolate in a bowl over hot water. Add 2 tablespoons of hot water and stir till smooth.

Halve the prunes lengthwise and stone.

To serve, put a spoonful of chestnuts on each plate, arrange 3 prune halves around the chestnuts and coat thickly with chocolate, decorating with whipped Jersey cream.

Chocolate Charlotte

La Ciboulette, Cheltenham
Chef/proprietor Kevin Jenkins

Serves 8–10

20 sponge fingers
1 vanilla sponge for the base
7 oz. (200g.) plain chocolate
6 fl. oz. (175g.) double cream,
  whipped
4 oz. (125g.) sugar
4 egg yolks
1 whole egg
6 leaves of gelatine
fresh custard

Line the base of a flan ring or charlotte mould with vanilla sponge and line the sides with the sponge fingers.

Melt the chocolate in a bowl over simmering water.

Beat the eggs in a machine till light and frothy.

Cook the sugar with a drop of water until 275F/140C, then pour onto the eggs beating all the time. Add the soaked gelatine and whisk until cool.

Fold the whipped cream into the chocolate and then add the egg mixture. Pour into the flan ring or charlotte mould and leave to set in the fridge. Serve with a fresh custard.

Chocolate and Chestnut Dessert

The Black Water Hotel, Colchester
Chef Robert Roudesli

Serves 8–10

1½ lbs. (700g.) chestnut purée
5½ oz. (160g.) unsalted butter
5½ oz. (160g.) caster sugar
7½ oz. (215g.) cooking chocolate
3 fl. oz. (75ml.) rum
Marrons glacé to decorate.

Beat the butter until light and creamy, gradually adding the caster sugar.

Melt the chocolate in a bowl over simmering water and allow to cool for 5 to 10 minutes.

Stir the chocolate into the sugar and butter mixture and gradually add the chestnut purée and the rum mixing until light and smooth. Line a 2 lb. (900g.) tin with lightly oiled greaseproof paper. Turn the mixture into the tin. Leave in the refrigerator over night. Turn out on a serving dish and decorate with cream and slices of marrons glacé.

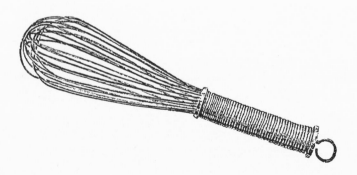

Sticky Chocolate Sweet

Tyrrells, Oundle
Chef Sara Jenson

Serves 8

8 oz. (225g.) plain chocolate
5 egg yolks, beaten
4 oz. (125g.) caster sugar
4 oz. (125g.) butter, melted
5 egg whites
8 oz. (225g.) savoy fingers
very strong black coffee
cream, whipped

Melt the plain chocolate in a bowl over simmering water until sticky. Cool slightly. Add the beaten egg yolks, caster sugar, and melted butter.

Beat the egg whites very stiffly and add to the mixture.

Dip the savoy fingers very quickly into very strong black coffee and press around the sides and bottom of a soufflé dish. Pour in the chocolate mixture. Cover with a small plate and put a weight on top. Chill for 24 hours.

Turn out and cover the top with whipped double cream and chill again before serving.

69

Iced

Bitter Chocolate Sorbet

Partners 23, Sutton
Chef/Proprietor Tim McEntire

Serves 4

6 oz. (175g.) best quality dark
   chocolate
6 oz. (175g.) caster sugar
½ pint (275ml.) water

This easy to make but interesting sorbet can be served in a little tuille biscuit basket with perhaps a white chocolate sauce, or simply in an attractive glass with a shortbread biscuit.

Gently melt the chocolate in a bowl over simmering water.

Make a light syrup with the sugar and the water.

Combine the two and churn in a sorbet ice-cream machine or simply place into the freezer. If using the freezer bring out from time to time and stir.

Chocolate and Cinnamon Sorbet

Popjoys, Bath
Chef/proprietor Ali Golden

Serves 6

1 lb. (450g.) sugar
6 oz. (175g.) Menier chocolate
   or other good dark chocolate
pinch salt
4 tablespoons rum
2 pints (generous litre) water
2 teaspoons coffee powder
½ teaspoon ground cinnamon
rum cream for decoration

Put the sugar, chocolate, salt, coffee, cinnamon, rum and water into a heavy bottom saucepan and bring slowly to the boil, stirring until the sugar is dissolved and you have a smooth consistency.

Continue to boil, stirring from time to time to stop it sticking to the bottom of the pan, until you have a good syrupy mixture (approximately 5 minutes). Then remove from the heat and cool.

Strain the liquid into the ice cream machine or freezer container. Turn in the ice cream maker until set or fast freeze until semi-frozen then remove from the freezer and whizz in a food processor to break up any crystals that have formed and return to the freezer till firm.

Serve decorated with whipped cream to which some rum has been added. For added bite little bits of chocolate can be stirred into the mixture before it is completely frozen to give a speckled effect.

Parfait au Chocolat

La Potinière, Gullane
Chef Hilary Brown

4 oz. (125g.) Bourneville
2 oz. (50g.) caster sugar
4 tablespoons cold water
½ pint (275ml.) double cream
3 egg yolks (size 2)
Tia Maria

Place the sugar and water in a small pan and bring to the boil. Once the sugar has dissolved boil for about 5 minutes. There should be 4 tablespoons left.

Meanwhile, break the chocolate into a liquidiser or food processor.

Whip the cream until it forms soft peaks.

Pour the hot syrup onto the chocolate, blend for 30 seconds, and then drop the yolks into the mixture. Continue to blend until the mixture lightens a little in colour, and becomes very smooth.

Empty the chocolate mixture onto the cream and using a balloon whisk mix them together until thoroughly blended.

Transfer to a jug and pour into 6–8 pot au crème dishes. Freeze for at least 3 hours.

Remove from the freezer 5–10 minutes before serving, and serve with a teaspoon of Tia Maria floating on the surface.

Parfait au Chocolat, Sauce Café

Priory Hotel, Bath
Chef Mike Collom

Serves 8

1 lb. (450g.) plain chocolate
½ pint (275ml.) double cream,
  half whipped
5 fl. oz. (150ml.) single cream
4 eggs
4 oz. (125g.) caster sugar
2 tablespoons rum

For the sauce:

4 egg yolks
½ pint (275ml.) single cream
1 teaspoon instant coffee
1 tablespoon Tia Maria
2 oz. (50g.) caster sugar

Make the parfait by melting the chocolate in a saucepan standing in hot water.

Whip the eggs and sugar until light and fluffy. To this, quickly add the melted chocolate and then fold in the half-whipped cream and lastly the rum. Pour into a tin-foil lined terrine mould. Place into deep freeze for 24 hours.

Make the sauce by whisking the egg yolks and sugar together. Bring the cream to the boil and pour onto the beaten yolks and sugar, whisking all the time. Still whisking, return to the pan and heat gently until the mixture thickens and coats the back of the spoon. Do not boil. Dissolve the instant coffee in the Tia Maria and add to the custard and allow to cool.

To serve, pour the coffee sauce on individual plates and then slice the parfait and lay on top. Decorate with whipped cream, any colourful fruit and a crisp biscuit.

Parfait of Two Chocolates

Thornbury Castle, Thornbury
Chef Colin Hingston

6 oz. (175g.) white chocolate
6 oz. (175g.) dark chocolate
6 fl. oz. (175ml.) cream
1 pint (575ml.) whipped cream

For the pâté à bombe:

5 fl. oz. (150ml.) egg yolk
5 fl. oz. (150ml.) hot water
10 oz. (275g.) caster sugar

Make the pâté à bombe by putting all the ingredients into a pan over simmering water. Cook until it thickens, stirring occasionally. When cooked, remove from heat and whisk until cool. It should double in volume.

To make the dark chocolate parfait melt the chocolate with 3 oz. (75g.) of cream. Fold the chocolate into 3 oz. (75g.) of the pâté à bombe and fold in ½ pint (275ml.) of the whipped cream. Half fill a terrine mould and place in the freezer. When almost set repeat the process with the white chocolate and fill the mould. Freeze.

To serve, turn out and serve slices with a coffee bean sauce

Chocolate and Coffee Ice Cream

Carved Angel, Dartmouth
Chef/proprietor Joyce Molyneux

Serves 6–8

8 oz. (225g.) Menier chocolate
3 oz. (75g.) ground coffee
½ pint (275ml.) milk
8 oz. (225g.) sugar
5 fl. oz. (150ml.) egg white
15 fl. oz. (425 ml.) double
  cream

Put the coffee in the milk and bring to the boil and infuse for 15 minutes. Strain through a muslin over chocolate broken into pieces. Mix till smooth.

Cook the sugar and egg whites over hot water to make a meringue. Remove from heat and beat till cool.

Whip the cream lightly.

When the chocolate mixture and meringue are cool, fold into the cream carefully. This mixture can be placed into a container and frozen without churning or piped into meringue cases and frozen. Serves well straight from the freezer.

Chocolate Iced Slice

Kenwards, Lewes
Chefs John Kenward & Jennie McWalter

Serves 10

Chocolate shortbread biscuit, cooked on baking sheet, cut into 2 pieces to fit the boxes in which the ice cream is frozen – cut biscuit while warm using a template

For the chocolate ice cream:

4 oz. (125g.) dark chocolate, melted
2 dessertspoons of cocoa
4 eggs, beaten and strained
2 oz. (50g.) caster sugar
½ pint (275ml.) double cream or whipping cream
few drops of vanilla extract
cupful of crème de cacao

For the chocolate 'glue':

2 tablespoons of cocoa
2 oz. (50g.) butter
8 tablespoons milk
4 tablespoons granulated sugar

Make the chocolate ice cream by beating the eggs with the sugar until very pale and much increased in bulk. Mix the cocoa into a paste with about 5 fl. oz. (150ml.) of boiling water. Cool. Whip the cream until fairly stiff. Fold the molten, but not too hot, chocolate and cooled cocoa mixture into the egg. Then fold in the cream. Add the vanilla and crème de cacao. Divide this mixture equally between 3 plastic boxes – approx. 10 x 30½" wide (25 x 8.5cm.) and freeze.

Make the chocolate glue by melting all the ingredients together gently and allow to simmer for a few minutes. Cool slightly.

To assemble: in a plastic box approximately 10 x 3½" wide (25 x 8.5cm.) 3½" deep (8.5cm.), assemble alternative layers of ice and shortbread, binding each with a thinly spread layer of the chocolate glue – starting and finishing with ice. Freeze again for some hours to bind, then turn out and slice. You can accompany with cream.

Warm Cherries with White Chocolate Ice Cream

Fischer's, Bakewell
Chef/proprietor Max Fischer

Serves 6

8 oz. (225g.) cherries, without
   stones
14 fl. oz. (400ml.) red wine
7 fl. oz. (200ml.) port
7 fl. oz. (200ml.) crème de
   cassis
2 tablespoons sugar
cornflour
zest and juice of 1 lemon
Kirsch

For the ice cream:

5 fl. oz. (150ml.) milk
5 fl. oz. (150ml.) cream
6 egg yolks
2 oz. (50g.) sugar
3½ oz. (100g.) white chocolate
   couverture

Caramelise the sugar in a pan. Add the zest of lemon and de-glaze with red wine. Reduce this liquid to half in quantity, add the brandy, cassis and cherries. Bring to the boil. Remove the cherries and thicken the stock with a little cornflour.

Return the cherries to the stock and add the lemon juice and a little Kirsch. Serve warm accompanied by the chocolate ice cream.

To make the chocolate ice cream. Place the milk, cream, chocolate and sugar into a pan. Bring to the boil. Thicken with egg yolk, but do not allow to boil again. Place the ice cream into an ice cream machine or into the freezer. If using a freezer bring out from time to time and stir. Serve with the cherries.

Iced Chocolate Cases with Rum Cream

Ballymaloe House, Shanagarry
Chef/proprietor Myrtle Allen

Makes 12 cases

8 oz. (225g.) chocolate
24 small cake cases
16 fl. oz. (450ml.) chocolate ice
  cream
9 fl. oz. (250ml.) whipped cream
1 teaspoon caster sugar
1 tablespoon rum

Spread a thin layer of melted chocolate inside a paper case of double thickness (i.e. one paper inside another). Allow to cool and set. Fill to the top with semi-frozen chocolate ice cream. Freeze until well set.

Peel off the papers. Top with a large rosette of whipped cream, lightly sweetened and flavoured with rum.

Iced Chocolate Terrine

Clos du Roy, Bath
Chef/proprietor Philippe Roy

Serves 8

6 egg yolks
8 oz. (225g.) caster sugar
8 oz. (225g.) Bourneville
1 pint (570ml.) whipping cream
4 oz. (125g.) walnuts, chopped
4 oz. (125g.) pistachio nuts,
  chopped

Mix the egg yolks and sugar until white. Melt the chocolate in a bowl over simmering water and mix with the egg and sugar.

Whip the cream until stiff and add to the mixture along with the walnuts and pistachio nuts. Put into a terrine and leave in the freezer for 6 hours to set.

Iced Chocolate, Brandy and Prune Terrine

Woods, Bath
Chef Mary Alley

Serves 6

3 eggs separated
2 oz. (50g.) sugar
3½ oz. (100g.) plain chocolate,
   melted in a bowl over
   simmering water
12 fl. oz. (350ml.) cream, softly
   whipped
armagnac

Line a 12" (30.5cm.) terrine tin with clingfilm.

Whisk the egg yolks and sugar until light and fluffy. Mix in the melted chocolate and fold this mixture into the softly whipped cream. Fold in stiffly whisked egg whites and a large measure of armagnac. Pour half of the mixture into the tin and top with a layer of prunes. Add the rest of the chocolate mixture, and fold clingfilm over the top and freeze.

When set, serve sliced with a vanilla sauce or hot chocolate sauce.

Pavé au Chocolat Sauce Vanille

Ortolan, Shinfield
Chef/proprietor J. W. Burton-Race

9 oz. (250g.) butter
9 oz. (250g.) chocolate
6 whole eggs
10 egg whites
7 oz. (200g.) cocoa powder
3½ oz. (100g.) sugar

For the sauce:

1 pint (570ml.) milk
8 egg yolks
2 oz. (50g.) sugar
vanilla pod

Melt the chocolate in a pan over simmering water.

Cream the butter with the cocoa powder. Add the egg yolks to the chocolate and then add the chocolate to the butter and cocoa powder.

Whisk the whites and when stiff add the sugar, then fold in the chocolate mixture and freeze in a mould. To serve, take out of freezer and leave in the fridge for about 20 minutes and serve with the vanilla sauce.

Make the sauce by boiling the milk and vanilla pod together. Cream the sugar and the yolks and then pour the milk onto the mixture and cook until it coats the back of the spoon – remove the vanilla pod.

Bombe Neluska

French Partridge, Horton
Chef/proprietor David Partridge

For the praline:

4 oz. (125g.) caster sugar
2 oz. (50g.) flaked almonds
2 oz. (50g.) crushed hazelnuts
4 tablespoons water

For the ice cream:

5 fl. oz. (150ml.) double cream
5 fl. oz. (150ml.) milk
2 egg yolks
1 oz. (25g.) caster sugar

For the bombe mixture:

2 egg yolks
2 oz. (50g.) caster sugar
1 oz. (25g.) cocoa powder
1 oz. (25g.) plain chocolate
2 fl. oz. (50ml.) water
4 fl. oz. (125ml.) cream

To make the praline, place the water and sugar in a heavy pan and bring to the boil and skim. Cook to a light caramel colour then add the nuts. Pour onto an oiled baking sheet. When quite cold crush with rolling pin and add to the ice cream.

To make the ice cream make a crème Anglaise in the usual way. Whip in the cream and freeze.

For the bombe mixture, make a syrup with the water and the sugar. Whisk in the egg yolks in a pan over boiling water, until cooked. Then add chocolate and cocoa. Cool. Whip cream and incorporate when the mixture is cold.

To make the bombe, first freeze the bombe mould and then line with praline ice cream layer by layer – freezing between each layer – until the required thickness. Pour the bombe mixture into the centre and cover with lid. Freeze.

Mount Vesuvius

Stane Street Hollow, Pulborough
Chef/proprietor Rene Kaiser

18 oz. (500g.) vanilla ice cream
3½ oz. (100g.) plain chocolate

For the praline:

5 oz. (150g.) sugar
3½ oz. (100g.) flaked almonds
little water

Melt the sugar with a little water and boil until a dark golden caramel. Remove from the heat and mix in the almonds. Pour the mixture on a sheet of tin foil and leave to cool. Chop finely with a large knife.

Allow the ice cream to soften a little and then mix in the chopped praline. Place into 4 individual moulds and return to the freezer.

Break up the chocolate and with a little water put into a bowl over simmering water and melt. Take the ice cream and nougat mixture from the moulds, allow to come round for about 10 minutes and then coat with the melted chocolate.

Iced Chocolate Oranges

Ballymaloe House, Shanagarry
Chef/proprietor Myrtle Allen

Serves 6

3–4 oranges
stock syrup
2 egg yolks
2 tablespoons sugar
1 pint (570ml.) whipped cream
1 level teaspoon powdered
  gelatine
1 oz. (25g.) plain chocolate
½ oz. (15g.) unsweetened
  chocolate

Cut the top off the oranges. Scoop out the pulp. Liquidise and sieve it and sweeten with syrup to taste. You will need ½ pint (275ml.) for the sweet.

Prepare an egg mousse as for vanilla ice cream. Divide it into two bowls. Melt the chocolate and add it to one bowl. Stir in half the whipped cream and half fill the oranges. Freeze.

Dissolve the gelatine in 1 tablespoon of orange juice over hot water. Blend with the measured orange and add to the remaining egg mousse. Fold in the cream and fill the oranges and return to the freezer. To serve, cut in quarters lengthwise and arrange on a serving dish decorated with orange segments, bay leaves and orange flavoured cream.

Cakes, Gateaux, Tarts etc

Chocolate Brandy Cake

Bowlish House, Shepton Mallet
Proprietors Julia and Brian Jordan

Serves 6–8

8 oz. (225g.) digestive biscuits
8 oz. (225g.) plain dark
chocolate
8 oz. (225g.) butter
3 oz. (75g.) caster sugar
2 eggs
2 oz. (50g.) walnuts
2 oz. (50g.) glacé cherries
brandy to taste, at least 6
tablespoons (whisky or rum
as alternatives)

Put the digestive biscuits into a freezer bag and pound until coarsely crushed.

Melt the chocolate and butter together in a bowl over simmering water.

Chop the glacé cherries into small pieces, crush the walnuts into similar sized pieces. Mix together.

Beat the eggs and sugar together and when creamy fold in the chocolate and butter mixture, followed by the walnut and cherry pieces and finally the crushed biscuits. Add the brandy or whisky. Pour this mixture into a buttered cake tin and allow to set in the fridge.

To remove for serving, stand the cake tin in hot water until the brandy cake starts to slightly melt around the rim. Place a large plate over the cake tin and invert – the cake should slide out of the tin onto the plate. Decorate to taste.

Chocolate Carrot Cake with Apricot Sauce

Gravetye Manor, East Grinstead
Chef Allan Garth

3 oz. (75g.) cake crumbs
11 oz. (300g.) carrot, grated
9 oz. (250g.) hazelnuts, grated,
  blanched and peeled
½ oz. (15g.) baking powder
1 tablespoon cinnamon
1½ tablespoons rum
1 lemon, grated
5 drops vanilla essence
5 egg yolks
4 oz. (125g.) caster sugar
4 tablespoons hot water
5 egg whites
4 oz. (125g.) caster sugar
chocolate to coat
marzipan to coat

For the apricot sauce:

1 lb. (450g.) fresh apricots,
  stoned
8 oz. (225g.) sugar
2 tablespoons apricot brandy
½ pint (275ml.) water

Note that this recipe cannot be halved or doubled.

Mix together the cake crumbs, grated carrot, hazelnuts and baking powder. Add the cinnamon, rum, lemon and vanilla essence.

Whisk the egg yolks, caster sugar and hot water to a high ribbon stage. Fold the egg yolk mixture into the carrot mixture. Whisk the egg whites and caster sugar to a meringue consistency, and fold into the carrot mixture. Pour into 9" (23cm.) baking tin and bake for 1 hour at 310F/160C/Gas 2½.

Cover the top of the cake with marzipan and brush with melted chocolate. Garnish with a marzipan, carrot and serve with an apricot sauce.

To make the apricot sauce, put the apricots, sugar and water into a thick bottomed pan and bring slowly to the boil. Cook until soft. Put the apricots into the liquidiser. Strain and add the apricot brandy and cool.

Chocolate Fudge Pudding

The Count House, Botallack
Chef Celia Reynolds

Serves 6

½ lb. (225g.) margarine
½ lb. (225g.) demerara sugar
4 eggs
10 oz. (275g.) self-raising flour
2 tablespoons cocoa
½ teaspoon vanilla essence
½ lb. (225g.) soft brown sugar
2 tablespoons cocoa

Cream together margarine and demerara sugar. Beat the eggs into the cream mixture. Fold in remaining ingredients and put into a buttered dish.

Combine the brown sugar and cocoa and quickly add two cups of boiling water. Pour over the sponge mixture. Place into oven 375F/190C/Gas 5 for 35–40 minutes.

Serve either hot with Cornish clotted cream – the fudge mixture is underneath the sponge – or cold with cherries or strawberries and cream.

Chocolate and Rum Gateaux

La Potinière, Gullane
Chef Hilary Brown

For the sponge:

2 eggs (size 2)
1½ oz. (40g.) caster sugar
2 level tablespoons cocoa
  powder

For the mousse:

8 oz. (225g.) Bourneville
  chocolate
5 fl. oz. (150ml.) unsalted butter
4 eggs (size 2)
3 tablespoons Jamaican Rum

For the sponge, set your oven at 350F/180C/Gas 4. Grease a 7" (18cm.) sandwich tin. Cut around the greaseproof paper to fit the base and grease also. Separate the eggs, placing both the yolks and the whites in medium sized bowls. Whisk the yolks with the sugar until the mixture starts to turn pale, then whisk in the sieved cocoa powder. Wash the beaters carefully, dry them, then whisk the whites until stiff. Carefully, but thoroughly, fold the whites into the chocolate mixture. Pour into the tin, level the surface, and bake in your pre-heated oven for 18 minutes. Remove from the oven, allow to cool for a few minutes and then carefully turn out to cool – turn out onto a clean dish towel then invert it back onto a cooling tray.

For the mousse, place the broken up Bourneville, butter and cream in a pirex which will fit over a pan of simmering water. Stirring occasionally, let the chocolate and butter melt completely. Remove the bowl from the pan, cool slightly then add the yolks and the rum. Mix together until smooth. Whisk the egg whites until stiff and then fold these into the chocolate mixture.

To finish the gateaux, cut the sponge in half, using a serrated bread knife. Place the bottom half in a 6½" (16.5 cm.) diameter, deep cake tin with a removable base. Pour the mousse mixture on top of the sponge and then place in the refrigerator for about an hour. Once it shows some signs of setting, carefully place the top layer of sponge on top. Leave to chill over night.

To serve, dust the gateaux with cocoa powder, place on a jar or similar and slide the cake tin downwards. Remove to a serving place and cut into wedges.

Chocolate Whisky Cake

Gravetye Manor, East Grinstead
Chef Allan Garth

7 oz. (200g.) marzipan

For the sponge:

3½. (100g.) sugar
5 egg yolks
2 fl. oz. (50ml.) Drambuie
2 oz. (50g.) ground almonds
2 oz. (50g.) grated chocolate
2 oz. (50g.) soft flour
4 egg whites

For the filling:

9 oz. (250g.) chocolate
3½ fl. oz. (100ml.) whisky
4 oz. (125g.) butter
9 fl. oz. (250ml.) cream

For the sauce:

8 egg yolks
18 fl. oz. (500ml.) milk
coffee essence
3 tablespoons sugar
1 fl. oz. (25ml.) coffee liqueur
3 tablespoons whipped cream

For the sponge, whisk the sugar and egg yolks to a sabayon. Mix in the Drambuie and ground almonds. whisk the egg whites and fold in the flour and grated chocolate. Mix all together. Spread out on 2 trays, 11 x 7" (28 x 18 cm.), on greaseproof paper. Bake at 400F/200C/Gas 6 for 8 minutes.

For the filling, gently melt the chocolate in a bowl over simmering water. Mix in the whisky, butter and cream. The mixture will go firm when cold.

To assemble, cut the sponge into 4 – you will now have 4 pieces of 11 x 3½" (28 x 9 cm.). Spread the softened chocolate mixture in 3 layers about ¼" (0.5 cm.) thick. Cover the cake with marzipan and finally coat with the chocolate mixture. Slice and serve on the coffee sauce.

To make the sauce, whisk the yolks, sugar and coffee liqueur in a bowl. Add the warm milk and cook over a bowl of hot water until it thickens. Cool and add the whipped cream.

For the sponge, whisk the sugar and egg yolks into a sabayon. Mix in the Drambuie and ground almonds. Whisk

Chocolate Chestnut Gateau

Thornbury Castle, Thornbury
Chef Colin Hingston

1 lb. (450g.) unsalted butter
4 oz. (125g.) caster sugar
3 egg yolks
1 lb. 12 oz. (825g.) dark
   chocolate
4 oz. (125g.) ground almonds
1 x 8 oz. (225g.) tin of
   sweetened chestnut purée
whole blanched almonds to
   garnish

Cream the butter, sugar and yolks together. Melt the chocolate in a bowl over simmering water.

Whisk the chocolate, almonds and chestnut purée into the creamed butter. Pour into two 7″ (18 cm.) flan tins. Leave to set.

To turn out, heat the side of the rings and push out from the base. Serve on the base with whole almonds pressed onto the sides.

Chocolate Nut Brandy Cake

The Country Garden, Ashburton
Chef Hassan El-Masri

1½ lbs. (700g.) dark chocolate
8 oz. (225g.) butter
2 fl. oz. (50ml.) sherry
1 fl. oz. (25ml.) brandy
2 fl. oz. (50ml.) rum
6 oz. (175g.) almonds (whole)
6 oz. (135g.) whole hazelnuts
6 oz. (175g.) whole brazil nuts

Melt the chocolate over a bain-marie.

When melted add the butter and mix in well. Add all the skinned nuts and alcohol and fold in. Pour into a 2lb. (900g.) loaf tin. Allow to set for three hours.

The chocolate will be soft enough to cut into thin slices without a hot knife. Serve with whipped cream and a fruit sauce.

Chocolate Mousse Meringue Gateau

Paul's, Folkestone
Chef/proprietor Penny Hagger

For the meringues:

6 egg whites
12 oz. (350g.) caster sugar

For the mousse:

11 oz. (300g.) dark chocolate
2 oz. (50g.) butter
6 eggs

Cadbury's Flake to decorate
whipped cream
icing sugar

To make the meringue, whisk the whites till light and frothy. Add the sugar at about intervals of 1 oz. (25g.) Divide the mixture equally into 4 and spread out onto a baking parchment making 4 similar circles. Place in the oven over night on the lowest heat setting possible.

To make the mousse, melt the dark plain chocolate in a bowl over simming water with the butter. Separate the eggs. Whisk the eggs until creamy and white in colour. Add the chocolate to the yolks and mix well being sure to mix in the chocolate thoroughly. Whisk the egg whites until light and fluffy. Fold the whites into the chocolate and yolk mixture. Allow to set firm in the refrigerator.

To assemble, form layers of the gateaux with firstly one meringue then the mousse and then the whipped cream. Do this until finishing with a layer of mousse. Decorate at the top with piped cream and Cadbury's Flakes and finish with a dusting of icing sugar.

The Meringue and Chocolate Layer Cake

Horn of Plenty, Gulworthy
Chef/proprietor Sonia Stevenson

For the meringue:

10 oz. (275g.) caster sugar
5 egg whites

For the filling:

9 oz. (250g.) bitter chocolate
  (Menier)
9 teaspoons coffee powder
3 packets unsalted butter
14 oz. (400g.) icing sugar
5 egg whites

Make the meringue mixture in the usual manner. Make 4 or 5 sheets of thin meringue (4″ x 8″) and dry out on silicone paper. (You can use a circular cake base as an alternative shape).

Make the filling mixture by putting the chocolate, coffee powder and 3 tablespoons of water in a saucepan and gently melt together. In a mixing bowl, cream the butter until soft and mix in the chocolate. In a double boiler put the egg whites and icing sugar and with an electric handbeater, whisk until hot and thick. Allow to cool a little and mix into the chocolate and butter mixture.

Layer the meringue sheets and the filling mixture alternately finally covering the outside with the mixture completely. Chill in the freezer for a minimum of 2 hours. Remove 20 minutes or so before cutting into slices or wedges.

Chocolate Truffle Cake

Sharrow Bay, Ullswater
Chef Alison Kennedy

5½ oz. (160g.) dark chocolate
2 teaspoons coffee powder
3½ oz. (100g.) butter
4½ oz. (140g.) caster sugar
4 eggs, separated
3½ oz. (100g.) toasted
   hazelnuts, ground

For the chocolate ganache:

5 oz. (150ml.) double cream
5 oz. (150g.) chocolate

For the chocolate icing:

6 oz. (175g.) chocolate
1 tablespoon water
1 oz. (25g.) butter

It is best to keep the cake for two days before cutting and filling, as it will otherwise be very crumbly.

Melt the chocolate with the coffee and 6 tablespoons water.

Cream the butter and sugar till pale. Beat in the egg yolks and fold in the chocolate and hazelnuts.

Whisk the egg whites till stiff and fold into the chocolate mixture. Pour into buttered 8½" (20cm.) tin. Cook at 325F/170C/Gas 3 for one hour and 15 minutes.

Make the ganache by bringing the cream to the boil, add broken chocolate, work till smooth, cool and lightly beat with a wooden spoon.

Make the icing by melting the chocolate and butter with the water.

To assemble, sandwich the cake with the ganache and coat with chocolate icing.

97

Chocolate Armagnac Loaf with Coffee and Walnut Liqueur Sauce

Thackeray's House Restaurant, Tunbridge Wells
Chef/proprietor Bruce Wass

1 sponge, soaked in armagnac
12 oz. (350g.) best bitter
  chocolate
½ pint (275ml.) double cream
1½ oz. (40g.) cocoa powder
½ coffee cup of armagnac
4 egg yolks
1 oz. (25g.) caster sugar
2 oz. (50g.) fresh butter, diced
½ pint (275ml.) cream, lightly
  whipped

For the sauce:

5 fl. oz. (150ml.) milk
4 egg yolks
2 oz. (50g.) caster sugar
1 dessertspoon coffee, freshly
  ground
walnut liqueur

In a double boiler melt the chocolate with the armagnac, double cream and cocoa powder.

Meanwhile, beat the egg yolks and caster sugar together until white and fluffy. Add the melted chocolate and the pieces of diced butter. Fold in the whipped cream.

Line a terrine mould with slices of the armagnac soaked sponge and fill with the chocolate mixture.

Leave to set in a refrigerator for at least six hours before slicing. Cut into ¾" (2cm.) slices and pour sauce around.

To make the sauce, bring the milk to the boil. Whisk the sugar and egg yolks together and pour on the milk. Thicken to a custard on the stove, stirring all the time and not allowing the mixture to boil. Add the coffee and leave to cool. Strain through a cloth and flavour with the walnut liqueur.

Chocolate Tart

Kenwards, Lewes
Chefs John Kenward & Jennie McWalter

1 x 9" (23 cm.) sweet shortcrust
   pastry flan case, baked blind
4 eggs
4 oz. (125g.) butter
2 oz. (50g.) demerara sugar
2 oz. (50g.) muscovada sugar
8 oz. (225g.) dark chocolate
2 level tablespoons cocoa
2 teaspoons instant coffee
vanilla extract
Cointreau

Melt the chocolate in a bowl over simmering water.

Melt the butter with the sugar in a basin over hot water.

Dissolve the cocoa and coffee in about 5 fl. oz. (150ml.) of boiling water.

Mix all together. Beat the eggs, strain and add to the mixture. Add a little vanilla extract and a cupful of Cointreau.

Cook in a low oven at 325F/170C/Gas 3 for 1–1½ hours until set firm. Serve cold with cream if desired.

Rich Chocolate Torte with Caramelised Butterscotch Sauce

Poole Court, Pool-in-Wharfedale
Chef Melvin Jordan

Serves 10–12

For the wholemeal sponge:

4 oz. (125g.) softened butter
2 medium size eggs
4 oz. (125g) soft brown sugar
2 level tablespoons baking
   powder, sieved together with
   4 oz. (125g.) wholemeal flour

For the vanilla sponge:

4 oz. (125g.) self raising flour
4 oz. (125g.) caster sugar
4 oz. (125g.) softened butter
2 medium size eggs

For each individual sponge, cream the butter and sugar until light in colour and texture. Add the eggs one at a time ensuring they are well mixed. Fold in the dry ingredients and pour into a square or round cake tin the size which will give approximately 1" (2.5 cm.) depth of mixture. Bake at 350F/180C/Gas 4 for approximately 15 minutes.

For the ganache, melt the chocolate being careful not to over heat it. Bring the cream, bay leaf and rum just to the boil. Remove the bay leaf. Pour the melted chocolate and cream mixture into the mixer bowl. Mix on a slow speed for a few seconds – then high until the cream begins to thicken. Finish for a few minutes on low speed. Remember to scrape the sides of the bowl frequently. When complete the mixture must be a stiff peak consistency.

When the sponges are cold, cut each into 3 thin equal layers, giving 9 layers in total. Brush off excess crumbs and sandwich each layer with a thin coat of ganache. You now have a complete slab or cake (the torte is best if left in the fridge overnight before serving it, and it will last for at least a week – in fact, it improves as the layers tend to become moist). To portion, cut a vertical slice approximately ½" (1 cm.) thick.

For the chocolate sponge:

3 oz. (75g.) self-raising flour
   sieved together with 1 oz.
   (25g.) cocoa powder
4 oz. (125g.) caster sugar
4 oz. (125g.) softened butter
2 medium size eggs

For the ganache:

8 oz. (225g.) plain Bourneville
   chocolate
5 fl. oz. (105ml.) double cream
1 bay leaf
1 teaspoon rum

For the butterscotch sauce:

8 oz. (225g.) butter
1–2 oz. (25–50g.) golden syrup
½ oz. (15g.) black treacle
1½ oz. (40g.) muscovado brown
   sugar
½ pint (275ml.) double cream

The gateau for my taste is best served slightly warmed – ideally a few seconds in the microwave or quickly flashed through the oven, but only for a very short time. Do not serve straight from the fridge. Serve with a hot caramelised butterscotch sauce.

To make the butterscotch sauce, melt the butter, syrup, treacle and sugar in a thick bottomed pan. Stir well. Bring slowly to the boil and boil for approximately 15 minutes until thick and quite dark. Remove from the heat and cool slightly. Pour in the cream slowly and combine well. Allow to cool.

Chocolate Marbled Tart

Hope End, Ledbury
Chef/proprietor Patricia Hegarty

Serves 8–10

For the pastry:

3 oz. (75g.) wholemeal flour
1½ oz. (40g.) unsalted butter
1 teaspoon icing sugar
1 teaspoon roasted and ground
   hazelnuts
3 tablespoons cold water

For the filling:

5 oz. (150ml.) strong bitter
   chocolate
¾ pint (400ml.) water
1 leaf of gelatine
2 egg whites
10 oz. (275g.) double cream

Make the pastry in the normal way and leave to rest for 20 minutes. Line a fluted 9½" (22cm.) flan ring with the pastry. Bake blind for 10 minutes at 400F/200C/Gas 6. Remove the filling and harden off for another 5 minutes in the oven.

Melt the chocolate in a bowl over hot water. Dissolve the gelatine in a ¼ pint (150ml.) of warm water and stir in the chocolate till smooth. Add the rum.

Whip the egg whites and then the cream and mix loosely together.

Cover the pastry base with a layer of chocolate. Put blobs of the cream mixture over this and swirl with a fork. Spoon over some more chocolate and continue with alternate layers finishing with the chocolate. Refrigerate.

N.B. It is important that the chocolate is cool but still runny. Too hot and it melts the cream, too cold and thick and it becomes too stiff to work.

Chocolate and Pineapple Cream Cake

The Count House, Botallack
Chef Celia Reynolds

Serves 8

6 oz. (175g.) plain chocolate
1 medium sized pineapple
¾ pint (400ml.) double cream,
    whipped until just taken
    shape
½ oz. (15g.) gelatine
5 fl. oz. (150ml.) pineapple juice
2 tablespoons chocolate liqueur

*For the crunch base and
topping:*

4 oz. (125g.) plain flour
4 oz. (125g.) butter
2 oz. (50g.) demerara sugar
2 oz. (50g.) hazelnuts, coarsely
    chopped

Rub together the plain flour and butter to resemble breadcrumbs. Combine all the ingredients of the crunchy base and bake on a baking sheet for 10 minutes at 400F/200C/Gas 6, or until brown. Leave to cool. Crush to make a crumble.

Finely chop the pineapple flesh, and reserve a little for decoration.

Melt the chocolate in a bowl over a pan of simmering water.

Dissolve the gelatine in the pineapple juice, and add the chocolate liqueur. Fold the ingredients together, adding the pineapple pieces last.

Use a spring clip or loose-bottomed tin 8″ (19cm.) in diameter. Starting with the crumble mix, layer with the cream mixture, finishing with the crumble top. Decorate with chocolate curls, whipped cream and pineapple.

Chill for a few hours. To serve, remove from the tin and slice as a cake.

Chocolate Cheesecake

Oakhill House, Nr Bath
Chef/proprietor Ann Long

For the chocolate case:

2 packets plain chocolate –
   Terrys or Bourneville
10" (25.5cm.) cake tin, with a
   loose bottom
tin foil
cling film

For the cheesecake:

6 oz. (175g.) chocolate – Terrys
   or Bourneville
2 tablespoons water
2 tablespoons Camp coffee
8 oz. (225g.) cream cheese
2 oz. (50g.) caster sugar
3 eggs
½ pint (275ml.) double cream
½ oz. (15g.) gelatine
2 tablespoons rum

This makes a light cheesecake served in a crisp chocolate casing.

Line the cake tin with foil, making sure to push it to the edges.

Break up the chocolate and put the pieces close together on a plate that will fit comfortably over a large saucepan. Half fill the open pan with water and bring to the boil. Switch off the heat, place the plate on top and leave until the chocolate melts. Put the plate on a dry tea towel (the plate bottom will be wet) and blend the chocolate together with a palette knife until smooth. Pour all the chocolate into the lined tin and spread it over using a pliable plastic spatula or the back of a spoon. Pay particular attention to the sides, where the chocolate will run back down until it begins to set. The chocolate should form a thick covering with no foil showing through. Leave the case to set for two hours, or better still overnight, in a cool place but not in the fridge.

Carefully lift the case out of the cake tin and peel the foil away from the chocolate. Line the cake tin with cling film and return the chocolate case.

Make the filling. Light the oven to the lowest setting. Place the rum and water into a small saucepan and sprinkle the gelatine evenly over. Leave to soak and melt at the very bottom of the oven – you should always be able to put your hand on the bottom of the pan as gelatine must melt slowly and not get too hot. Leave alone for about five minutes and it will be ready to use.

Break the chocolate into a small saucepan and add water and Camp coffee. Melt over a low heat, stirring all the time until you have a smooth chocolate cream. Remove from the heat, stir in the melted gelatine and pour the chocolate into a jug. Separate the eggs, putting the whites into a large mixing bowl and the yolks into the food processor with the cream cheese and sugar: work until smooth. Set the blender in motion again, pour in the double cream and blend. Whisk the egg whites till stiff. Start the blender again and pour in the chocolate and work till smooth. Gently fold the cheese chocolate into the egg whites, using a metal spoon to prevent the breaking down of the air bubbles. Pour the mixture into the chocolate case. Leave to set in the refrigerator.

Chocolate and Walnut Cheesecake

Ston Easton Park, Ston Easton
Chef M. Harrington

For the base:

2 oz. (50g.) butter, melted
¾ packet Digestive biscuits, broken

For the topping:

8 oz. (225g.) plain couverture chocolate
8 oz. (225g.) Philadelphia cream cheese
4 oz. (125g.) walnuts, chopped
½ oz. (15g.) gelatine
3 oz. (75g.) caster sugar
3 eggs (no. 3)
½ pint (275ml.) double or whipping cream

Mix the melted butter with the broken biscuits to make a base for an 8 x 9" (20.5 x 23cm.) ring.

Dissolve the gelatine in two tablespoons of water. Add the chocolate and leave to melt. Allow to cool but not set.

Beat the egg yolks and sugar. Add the cheese and beat until smooth. Add the chocolate mixture and then the lightly whipped cream and walnuts and fold in the egg whites. Place the mixture on the base and leave to set.

Cassata alla Siciliana

The Wife of Bath, Wye
Chef/proprietor Bob Johnson

Serves 12

1 fresh sponge cake, 3 x 3 x 9"
(7.5 x 7.5 x 23cm.) long
8 oz. (225g.) soft cream cheese
½ pint (275ml.) double cream
2 oz. (50g.) caster sugar
4 oz. (125g.) mixed nuts,
chopped
2 oz. (50g.) grated chocolate
2½ tablespoons Strega or
orange flavoured liqueur
zest of one lemon or orange

For the chocolate icing:

8 oz. (225g.) bitter chocolate
6 tablespoons strong coffee
6 oz. (175g.) butter, chilled and
cut into cubes

Slice the sponge cake horizontally into ½ to ¾" (1–2.0cm.) slices.

Beat the cheese, cream and liqueur until smooth. Stir in the fruit, nuts, chocolate and zest and mix together.

Lay one slice of sponge on a plate and cover with a thick layer of the mixture. Add another slice of sponge and so on until all the sponge mixture is used up. Smooth sides and make compact. Refrigerate for about 2 hours.

For the icing, melt the chocolate and coffee in a double saucepan until smooth. Remove from heat and beat in butter. Beat until the mixture is smooth and allow to cool until spreading consistency.

Using a palette knife spread the mixture evenly on all sides and top of gateaux. Then using a piping bag put swirls of icing on the top and sides to decorate. Refrigerate over night before serving.

A Clos du Roy Special

Clos du Roy, Bath
Chef/proprietor Philippe Roy

Serves 8

For the dacquoise:

10 egg whites
14 oz. (400g.) caster sugar
11 oz. (300g.) ground almonds

For the bavaroise:

18 fl. oz. (500ml.) milk
4 oz. (125g.) egg yolk
5 oz. (150g.) caster sugar
18 oz. (500g.) couverture
   chocolate
4 leaves gelatine
23 fl. oz. (650ml.) whipping
   cream

Make the dacquoise by whisking the egg whites until stiff. Add 3½ oz. (100g.) of the caster sugar, still whisking. Mix the ground almond with the rest of the sugar and fold into the stiff egg white. Cook in the oven at 425F/220C/Gas 7 for 15 minutes in a thin layer on a buttered baking tray.

Bring the milk to the boil. Whisk the yolk and sugar until the mixture becomes white. Add the boiling milk and cook slowly until the mixture thickens. Do not reboil. Filter the mixture through a sieve and mix in the chocolate. Add four leaves of gelatine and cool down. Whip the cream until stiff and add to the mixture. Allow to cool down until the mixture becomes a thick paste.

Cut the biscuit into 2 rounds, one bigger than the other. Place the mixture onto the smaller biscuit in the form of a dome. Cover with the larger biscuit and decorate with flaked almonds and chocolate powder.

Marjolaine

Le Coq Hardi, Dublin
Chef/proprietor John Howard

1 lb. (450g.) almonds, blanched
10 oz. (275g.) hazelnuts
1 lb. (450g.) granulated sugar
16 egg whites
1 lb. (450g.) bitter chocolate, broken into small pieces
2 oz. (50g.) grated dark chocolate
8 tablespoons unsalted butter
1 pint (570ml.) double cream
1 pint (570ml.) crème chantilly
1 tablespoon icing sugar

Spread the almonds and hazelnuts on two separate baking trays. Toast the almonds in an oven till golden, and the hazelnuts till their skins begin to pucker – rub them in a coarse cloth till they come off completely. Mix the nuts together, add the sugar and grind very finely. Set aside one quarter of this mixture.

Beat the egg whites till they stand in peaks. Fold in the nuts. Butter a baking tray and spread the mixture into a 12 x 16" (30.5 x 40.5cm.) rectangle ¼" (0.5cm.) thick and smooth it with a spatula. Bake in the oven at 400F/200C/Gas 6 for 30 minutes. Cool and cut into 4 strips 12 x 4" (30.5 x 10cm.).

Melt the chocolate in a double boiler over a low heat, adding the butter bit by bit, stirring constantly. Remove from the heat and cool slightly. Whip the cream and fold it into the chocolate. Chill before using.

Cover one of the meringue strips with a layer of chocolate cream and place a second strip on top. Mix the crème chantilly with the reserved nuts and spread on top of the meringue. Cover with the third strip of meringue and another layer of chocolate cream and then the last strip of meringue. Sprinkle with icing sugar and grated chocolate. Smooth the remaining chocolate cream over the sides of the cake and refrigerate for 24 hours before serving.

Chocolate and Almond Rum Cake

Cannons, Bath
Chef Raymond Duthie

9 oz. (250g.) bitter chocolate
3 fl. oz. (75ml.) rum
9 oz. (250g.) unsalted butter
7 oz. (200g.) caster sugar
6 eggs, separated
2 tablespoons caster sugar
7 oz. (200g.) ground almonds
6 oz. (175g.) plain flour

For the topping:

4 oz. (125g.) unsalted butter
4 oz. (125g.) bitter chocolate
2 tablespoons rum

Melt the chocolate and rum together. Cream the butter and sugar till light and fluffy. Add the egg yolks slowly and beat well. Stir in the chocolate and almonds.

Beat the egg whites and extra sugar and fold into the rest of the mix with the flour. Pour into a well greased and lined 10" (25cm.) cake tin and bake for 50 minutes in a medium oven.

When cold spread the top and sides with the topping which you have melted together. Spread the sides with toasted flaked almonds and decorate with crystallized violets. This cake is delicious eaten with a few fresh strawberries.

Sacher Torte

Billesley Manor, Billesley
Chef Michael Monahan

7 oz. (200g.) butter
3 oz. (75g.) caster sugar
5 egg yolks
5 oz. (150g.) chocolate
7 oz. (200g.) cinnamon
½ lemon zest
5 egg whites
3 oz. (75g.) sugar
4 oz. (125g.) apricot jam

For the ganache:

14 oz. (400g.) chocolate
2 oz. (50g.) sugar
2 oz. (50g.) butter
5 fl. oz. (150ml.) milk
5 fl. oz. (150ml.) cream

Grease and flour a sponge ring. Beat the butter and sugar until light and fluffy. Melt the chocolate in a bowl over simmering water and add a few drops of water. Gradually add the egg yolks to the butter mixture, followed by the melted chocolate. Continue beating.

Meanwhile whisk the egg whites and sugar. Fold this meringue into the mixture. Sift the flour and cinnamon and fold into the mixture. Pour into a greased sponge ring and bake at 350F/180C/Gas 4. When cooked, cool and cut into two. Sandwich with apricot jam. Boil up some apricot jam and brush all over.

Make the ganache and pour over the sponge. Place in the fridge to set. Decorate by melting some chocolate and signing the top of the cake 'Sacher'.

Petits Fours

Ballymaloe Chocolates

Ballymaloe House, Shanagarry
Chef/proprietor Myrtle Allen

2 oz. (50g.) softened chocolate
12–14 strawberries or grapes
6 tablespoons stock syrup
6 tablespoons kirsch

Smear the chocolate onto petits fours cases. They should be of double thickness (i.e. one case inside the other). Chill and peel off the paper carefully. It is a good idea to keep some melted chocolate handy for patching, should a crack appear.

Wash, dry and hull the strawberries and cut in rounds – alternatively peel and remove pips from grapes. Put the fruit in a cup and pour over the syrup and kirsch and leave to soak for 10 minutes. Fill the chocolate cases with fruit and pour over the syrup. Serve on a paper doyley within 2 hours.

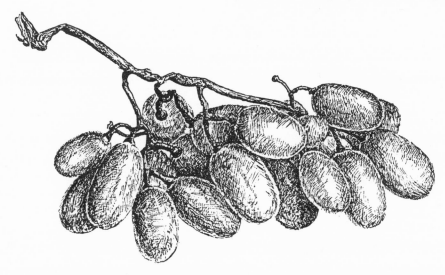

Rum Truffles

The Peat Inn, Peat Inn
Chef/proprietor David Wilson

Enough for 12 people

6 oz. (125g.) good quality plain
dark chocolate
1 egg yolk
¾ oz. (20g.) unsalted butter
2 fluid oz. (50ml.) double cream
1 fluid oz. (25ml.) dark navy rum
cocoa powder

Break the chocolate into a saucepan. Place the saucepan in a bain-marie over a larger saucepan with a little water in it. Stir occasionally over heat until the chocolate is melted, and smooth. Take the pan off the heat.

Add the butter to the pan in small pieces. Stir until melted. Add the egg yolk, cream and rum and beat for 5 minutes. Refrigerate or place in freezer to set quicker.

To make the truffles, spoon a small amount of mixture out of the bowl, roll into a ball and then roll in cocoa powder. Place in a little paper case. Refrigerate. Keep the truffles refrigerated until required to serve with coffee. This mixture will keep very well refrigerated.

Rum Truffles

Homewood Park, Hinton Charterhouse
Chef/proprietor Stephen Ross

approximately 30 truffles

6 oz. (175g.) plain chocolate
¾ oz. (20g.) soft butter
1 egg yolk
1 fl. oz. (25ml.) rum
4 oz. (125g.) icing sugar
chocolate vermicelli

Melt the chocolate in a double saucepan. Stir in the butter and egg yolk. Add the rum and mix well. Fold in the icing sugar.

To make the truffles, form into small balls, coat with vermicelli and place in paper. Place in a refrigerator until required.

White Chocolate Macadamia

Hall of Plenty, Gulworthy
Chef/proprietor Sonia Stevenson

macadamia nuts
white chocolate
Pernod
blanchor Lindt chocolate (with
   coconut pieces and a
   crunch)

Blanch the macadamia nuts to get rid of the salt.

Melt the white chocolate in a bowl over simmering water.
Mix in enough Pernod to make a fudge.

Coat the nuts in the fudge and cool.

Melt the Lindt chocolate in a pan over simmering water.
Cover the coated nuts in the melted Lindt and allow to set
in the refrigerator.

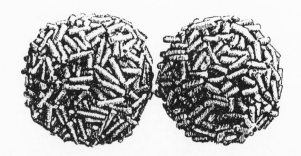

White Chocolate Praline Petit Four

Buckland Manor, Buckland
Chef Martyn Pearn

Quantity approximately 16

6 oz. (175g.) white chocolate
½ wine glass of armagnac
6 fl. oz. (175ml.) double cream
3 oz. (75g.) blanched almonds
6 oz. (175g.) caster sugar

Melt the chocolate in a bain-marie.

Make the praline by caramelising the sugar and almonds together. Pour onto a cold slab, preferably marble, and allow to cool. Grind when cold.

Bring the cream to the boil and add the melted chocolate. Whisk until cool. Add the praline to the chocolate and pipe into small rosettes onto greased-proof paper.

Chocolate Coconut Balls

Tyrrells, Oundle
Chef Sara Jenson

Serves 4

½ lb. (225g.) plain chocolate
¾ cup of sweetened
   condensed milk
1 cup walnuts, chopped
1 cup dates, chopped
1 cup sultanas
desiccated coconut

Melt the plain chocolate in a bowl over hot water. Remove from heat and stir in the sweetened condensed milk, the walnuts, dates, and the sultanas. Mix well.

Roll the mixture into balls and coat in desiccated coconut. Leave to harden in the fridge. These will be best after 24 hours.

Chocolate Nougat Petit Four

Restaurant Seventy Four, Canterbury
Chef/proprietor *I. L. Mcandrew*

To make 60 pieces

12 oz. (350g.) milk chocolate
8 oz. (225g.) nougat paste
6 oz. (175g.) dark chocolate

Line a tray approximately 8 x 10 x 1" (20 x 25 x 2.5 cm.) with greased-proof paper. Melt the milk chocolate in a bowl over a bath of hot water. Add the nougat paste and stir in well. Pour this into the tin and allow to set.

When set turn out onto a board.

Cut the dark chocolate into small pieces and melt into a bowl over a bath of hot water, not allowing the chocolate to become any hotter than blood temperature.

Spread half of the dark chocolate over one side of the milk chocolate and the nougat slab and allow to set. When set turn the slab over and repeat the process. Decorate the second side by running over it with a comb scraper or a fork. Allow to set again. When firmly set cut into oblongs about 1½ x ¾" (4 x 2 cm.)

Chocolate Covered Strawberries

Paul's Restaurant, Folkestone
Chef/proprietor Penny Hagger

3½ oz. (100g.) plain flour
1 oz. (25g.) butter
4 tablespoons double cream
strawberries as required
icing sugar to dust

Melt the plain chocolate in a bowl over simmering water with the butter. When the chocolate has melted add the double cream until the chocolate appears glossy, yet still dark and able to coat the back of the spoon thickly.

Leaving the green stalks on and holding by the stalks, dunk the strawberries into the chocolate making sure of an even coat all over. Shake off any excess and place on baking parchment, and pop into the fridge until set. To serve, dust with icing sugar.

Small Chocolate and Chestnut Meringues

The White House, Williton
Chef/proprietor Kay Smith

2 oz. (50g.) chocolate
double cream, whipped
small tin of sweetened chestnut
    purée

The meringue mix:

4 egg whites
8 oz. (225g.) caster sugar

When making meringues add a couple of dozen small swirls ½–¾″ (1–1.5cm.) in diameter onto greaseproof paper and bake in a low oven. When cooked dip the ends in melted bitter chocolate.

You can keep these excellent petits fours to use as required. Serve by sandwiching two together with a mixture of whipped cream and sweetened chestnut purée.

Rich Chocolate Cake Squares

The Old Manor House, Romsey
Chef/proprietor Mauro Bregoli

1 x 12" (30.5cm.) round sponge
   tin
9 oz. (250g.) plain chocolate
9 oz. (250g.) butter
6 eggs
3½ oz. (100g.) plain flour, sifted
7 oz. (200g.) powdered
   almonds
8 oz. (200g.) caster sugar

This cake has an intense chocolate flavour and should be served cut into small squares as petits fours.

Set your oven to maximum heat.

Over a low heat, in a bain-marie, beat together the sugar and the eggs until warm.

In another bowl, over simmering water, mix the chocolate and butter together until they thicken. Slowly fold in the powdered almonds and the sifted flour. Finally the sugar and egg mixture.

Pour the mixture into a lightly greased cake tin, turn down the heat and bake in a moderate oven until the sponge is springy to the touch (approximately 20 minutes). When cool cut into small squares and serve as petits fours.

Notes

Drybridge

Peat Inn

Gullane

Ullswater

Windermere

Pool in Wharfdale

Kenilworth

Dublin

Bakewell

Loughborough

Llandudno

Oundle

Bishops Tachbrook

Gorey

Diss

Horton

Malvern Wells

Corse Lawn

Buckland

Stratford-on-Avon

Shanagarry

Ledbury

Colchester

Llandewi Skirrid

Wye

Bicester

Cheltenham

Bristol

London

Bath

East Grinstead

Oakhill

Canterbury

Ston Easton

Haslemere

Folkestone

Williton

Romsey

Pulborough

Ashburton

Lewes

Tunbridge Wells

Chagford

Shepton Mallet

Hinton Charterhouse

Botallack

Dartmouth

Gulworthy

Jersey

Restaurant Addresses

Ballymaloe House	– Shanagarry, Co. Cork.	Cork 652531
Billesley Manor	– Billesley, Nr. Stratford-upon-Avon.	0789 763737
Blackwater Hotel	– 20–22 Church Road, Colchester.	0206 38 3338
Restaurant Bosquet	– 97a Warwick Road, Kenilworth.	0926 52463
Bowlish House	– Shepton Mallet, Somerset.	0749 2022
Buckland Manor	– Buckland, Gloucestershire.	0386 852626
Cannons	– Bath, Somerset.	0225 834644
Carved Angel	– 2 South Embankment, Dartmouth.	08043 2465
La Ciboulette	– 24–26 Suffolk Road, Cheltenham.	0242 573449
Le Coq Hardi	– 35 Pembroke Road, Dublin.	Dublin 689070
Corse Lawn House	– Corse Lawn, Gloucestershire.	045278 479
Count House	– Botallack, Penzance.	0736 788588
Country Garden	– 22 East Street, Ashburton, Devon.	0364 53431
L'Escargot	– 48 Greek Street, London W1.	01 437 2679
Fischer's	– Woodhouse, Bath Street, Bakewell.	062 981 2687
Flowers	– 27 Monmouth Street, Bath.	0225 313774
Fox & Goose	– Fressingfield, Diss, Norfolk.	037986 247
French Partridge	– Horton, Nr. Northampton.	0604 870033
Gidleigh Park	– Chagford, Devon.	064 73 2367
Gravetye Manor	– Sharpthorne, Nr. East Grinstead.	0342 810567
Hilaire	– 68 Old Brompton Road, London.	01 584 8993
Homewood Park	– Hinton Charterhouse, Bath.	022 122 2643
Hope End	– Ledbury, Hereford & Worcester.	0531 3613
Horn of Plenty	– Gulworthy, Nr. Tavistock.	0822 832528
Kenwards	– 151a High Street, Lewes, Sussex.	0273 472343
Longueville Manor	– Jersey, Channel Islands.	0534 25501
Marlfield House	– Gorey, Co. Wexford.	Gorey 21124
Michael's	– 129 Hotwell Road, Bristol.	0272 276190
Morels	– 25 Lower Street, Haslemere, Surrey.	0428 51462
Oakhill House	– Oakhill, Bath.	0749 840180

Old Manor House	– 21 Palmerston Street, Romsey.	0794 517353
Ortolan	– Old Vicarage, Shinfield, Berkshire.	0734 883783
Partners 23	– 23 Stonecot Hill, Sutton.	01 644 7743
Paul's	– 2a Bouverie Road West, Folkestone.	0303 59697
The Peat Inn	– Peat Inn, Fife.	033 484 206
Pool Court	– Pool in Wharfedale, West Yorkshire.	0532 842288
Popjoys	– Sawclose, Bath.	0225 60494
La Potinière	– Gullane, East Lothian.	0620 843214
Le Poulbot	– 45 Cheapside, London EC2.	01 236 4379
Priory Hotel	– Weston Road, Bath.	0225 331922
Restaurant Roger Burdell	– Manor House, Loughborough.	0509 231813
Roger's	– 4 High Street, Windermere, Cumbria.	096 62 4954
Royal Crescent Hotel	– Royal Crescent, Bath.	0225 319090
Restaurant Seventy-Four	– 74 Wincheap, Canterbury.	0227 67411
Sharrow Bay	– Honiton Road, Ullswater, Cumbria.	085 36 301
Stane Street Hollow	– Pulborough, West Sussex.	07982 2819
Ston Easton Park	– Ston Easton, Somerset.	076121 631
Thackeray's House	– 85 London Road, Tunbridge Wells.	0892 37558
Thornbury Castle	– Thornbury, Nr. Bristol.	0454 412647
Tyrrells	– 6 & 8 New Street, Oundle.	08322 2347
White House	– Williton, Somerset.	0984 32306
Wife of Bath	– 4 Upper Bridge Street, Wye.	0233 812540
Woods	– 9–13 Alfred Street, Bath.	0225 314812
Woods	– Bignell View, Bicester.	08692 41444

Index